THE
CREATION
OF
ATOMS
AND
STARS

THE
CREATION
OF
ATOMS
AND
STARS

David E. Fisher

illustrations by
John A. Nez

Holt, Rinehart and Winston
NEW YORK

Other books by David E. Fisher

NOVELS:
Crisis
A Fearful Symmetry
The Last Flying Tiger

NONFICTION:
Creation of the Universe

Library of Congress Cataloging in Publication Data
Fisher, David E.   1932-   The creation of atoms and stars.
Bibliography: p.   Includes index.
SUMMARY: Discusses the creation and activity
of atoms and stars.
1. Stars—Evolution—Juvenile literature.
2. Cosmochemistry—Juvenile literature.
[1. Stars—Evolution.   2. Universe] I. Title. QB806.F57
523.8   79-4469   ISBN 0-03-046511-7

For my parents,
Grace S. and Henry R. Fisher

Contents

✡ I ✡

The
Problem

Many thousands of years ago, when people first began to crawl out of their caves and look at the world around them and wonder about it, what were some of the first questions they asked themselves? The first ones probably were: "What is that sun? What keeps it burning so bright day after day?" And then: "What are those stars at night? What keeps them burning night after night?" And then, looking more closely at the world, at the trees and the grass, at the animals and at themselves, at their own fingers and toes: "What are *we* made of? Why is a rock different from an eyeball? What is the grass made of and what am *I* made of?"

Many thousands of years went by and whole generations lived and died and nobody had the faintest answer to any of these questions. In fact, nobody even suspected the basic truth, which is that all of these questions have the same answer!

People didn't even know how to *begin* to find the answer. They tried religion and they tried superstition, they tried astrology and alchemy and witchcraft and they even tried asking their parents, and all of these gave answers but all the answers were wrong. Finally, as a last resort, they began to use their own brains.

They began to put together *theoretical models* of the universe. Such models, existing only in the mind, are a sensible way to go about attacking a problem which can't be solved directly. As long as you can't pick up a piece of a star and examine it, you can't be sure exactly what it is made of. So you put together in your mind a picture of what it *might* be; you imagine a "model" which describes the stars and their relation to the universe. And you then go on and imagine what the consequences of your model might be: how the stars would behave if your theoretical model were really true. If the consequences of the model appear similar to how the stars are actually observed to behave, you begin to accept the model. If further observations are made which the model is incapable of explaining, you either throw away the model or try to modify it to incorporate these new facts.

For example, one of the first models to explain the existence of the stars was that the stars didn't *really* exist. They were only small holes, tears in the fabric of the sky. This model pictured the earth as being in the center of the universe, surrounded by a sort of dark inverted bowl which is the sky. During the day the sun comes by and lights up the inside of this bowl and it appears to us to be blue. At night when the sun disappears, it is of course simply black. On the other side of this inverted bowl lies heaven, and at night the glorious light of heaven leaks through to us through small holes in the inverted bowl of the sky.

This makes sense at first. It explains why the sky is blue in the day and dark at night, with these little pinpricks of light in it. The next fact to be observed was that the stars are in the same place every night, and this also fits the model; we see the stars wherever there is a hole in the fabric of the sky, and the position of these holes should not change from day to day (or rather from night to night).

The next fact to be observed was that actually the stars did *not* stay still, but revolved around the earth. If you sit outside at night for a few hours and watch the stars, you can see them moving slowly across the sky just as the sun does during the daytime. This observation could also be made to fit the model; it only had to be modified slightly so that the inverted bowl which was the sky revolved around the earth. Then although the light of heaven is constant, the holes through which we see this light must necessarily revolve around us.

It's a very nice little model and it worked very well—until people discovered the planets. These planets, discovered by the Greeks a couple of thousand years ago, consist of objects in the sky that looked exactly like the normal stars except that they wandered from place to place (Figure 1). They noticed that one night a group of stars might appear as they do in Figure 1 (a), but perhaps a month later they would appear as in Figure 1 (b); the stars A, B, C, and D maintained their respective positions and could easily be thought of as holes in the fabric of the sky, but the star X wandered away from the other four. They found five of these wandering stars (the Greek word for wanderer is *planet*) and realized there was no way to modify the model

Figure 1. A group of stars A,B,C,D and a planet X, seen in (a) and (b) at different times of the year. The stars keep their relative positions, but the planet has moved.

to incorporate this new observation. Nobody could think of a way in which holes could wander from place to place from night to night, and so they had to acknowledge that the model must be wrong. A new model would have to be constructed.

Not much progress was made for the next thousand years or so, until the time of Copernicus, when we finally put together another model. By this time it was recognized that there is a basic difference between the planets and the stars; the stars are bodies that generate their own light and shine out into the sky, and the planets are cold bodies which only reflect the light of a nearby star. In the Copernican model, the sun is recognized as a star which appears brighter than the other stars only because it is so much closer to us. And around this star all the planets revolve, including our own earth, absorbing light and heat from the sun and reflecting some of it back into the sky.

This model of our solar system actually seems to be true; there are no observations which conflict with it. And one of the lovely things about such theoretical models is that they not only correlate and explain our observations, but frequently they lead us on in new directions. And so it is with this Copernican model. For if the sun is actually a star, and much closer to us than any other star, we might be able to make careful observations of the sun and from such observations put together a model which will describe *all* the stars. In particular, we wonder what makes the sun—and the stars—shine. What is actually burning inside the stars and the sun, producing the light and heat that make possible all life on earth?

❖2❖
A
Question
of Time

Although the energy coming out of the sun is tremendously large, it is not difficult to understand it if the sun has only existed for a short period of time. In fact, if the sun were composed of a material similar to those that can burn on earth, and if it were burning by the same kind of fire—if the sun were, for example, one gigantic charcoal fire—it would be *such* a gigantic charcoal fire that it could easily maintain the energy that we observe coming from its surface for many hundreds of years, perhaps even for thousands of years. So if the sun is only a few hundred years old, or even a few thousand, there would be no problem. But how old is the sun, really?

The first attempts to answer this question were based on legend, mythology, superstition, or religion. In the Middle Ages people who took the Bible literally attempted to calculate the age of the universe by adding up all the generations of man described there. By estimating an average age for each generation, they were able to calculate when man was created. After that it was simply a question of adding six days to the result to arrive at when the universe was created. The most widely accepted result of this line of reasoning was that of Archbishop Ussher, who in the 17th century came to the conclusion that the universe was created in the year 4004 B.C., on Sunday, the 23rd of October.

Of course, such an exact pinpointing of the time is not possible with the information contained in the Bible, even if it were true. The Archbishop went a little overboard on his model, as perhaps physicists do today on theirs. But certainly it was true that if one took the Bible as the literal word of God a simple calculation indicated that the universe was a few thousand years old, no more than that. If that were true, it meant that the sun could be understood in terms of the type of phenomena we observe on earth; the fire lighting the sun was nothing mysterious, but simply a normal fire— although certainly a very big one.

However, as time went on, not many scientists were willing to accept the Bible as the literal truth of the natural universe, for obvious reasons, and they began to look for independent methods of estimating the age of the sun. The next major advance came about gradually over the next two hundred years, when we came to realize that there is no way the earth could have been created independently of the sun. The solar system consists almost entirely of the sun: 98% of all the material contained in the sun, planets, asteroids, meteorites, and comets is in fact contained in the sun itself. In general terms, the sun *is* the solar system; all the rest of it—comets, meteorites, moons, and planets—is little more than an afterthought. So whenever people tried to figure out how the solar system could have been created, they came again and again to the conclusion that all of the planets must have been created somehow in conjunction with the sun. There is no agreement precisely as to how this was done, but it is clear that the planets in general and the earth in particular could not have existed by themselves before the sun was created. Therefore the problem of the age of the sun can be reworded into the problem of the age of the earth: the sun is at least as old as the earth.

This simplifies things a good deal: instead of trying to estimate the age of a ball of fire in the sky which no one can approach or sample, we now have the alternative but equivalent problem of estimating the age of the earth on which we live, the earth which we can sample directly and upon which we can make direct measurements.

So all right then, here you sit on this earth: how are you going to measure how long it might have existed?

Well, you might look at the earth and wonder how it got to be this way. For example, the oceans are salty, aren't they? Did you ever wonder why? Let's construct a theoretical model.

The observation we have to explain with our model is first, that the oceans are salty, and second, that rivers and lakes are not. A workable model might go like this:

The oceans are fed by the mighty rivers of the earth: the Amazon, the Missouri and the Mississippi, and a dozen others around the globe, which descend from lakes and pour and tumble through the continents on their way to the ocean basins. But if the rivers are continuously running from the lakes into the oceans, why don't the lakes eventually empty and the oceans overflow? Because there is an opposite process going on. The water sitting in the oceans is continually being evaporated by the sun, just as water from a plate set outside in the sun will evaporate and disappear. In the case of the oceans the water does not disappear, but rises into the atmosphere where it forms clouds (of course the water from the plate also does this, but is too little to be noticed). These clouds then rain on the oceans and on the continents. The part that rains upon the oceans has no noticeable effect. This is simply water that has evaporated from the oceans and then is returned directly to them. But the water that rains upon the continents ends up in lakes and rivers and from here runs again back into the oceans. We have therefore a continuous cycle of never-ending transportation of water from the continents to the oceans to the atmosphere and back to the continents as in Figure 2.

What does such a model have to do with *salty* oceans? Suppose that the rivers are not actually 100% fresh. Suppose that as they wash over the continental rocks and soil they dissolve minute quantities of salt and carry the salt down to the oceans. And suppose that the salt does not then evaporate into the atmosphere when the ocean water does.

If these suppositions are true, then fresh water would be cycled continuously between the lakes and oceans and back again, while the minute quantities of salt would be fed continuously into the oceans and would *remain* there. The oceans would there-

Figure 2.

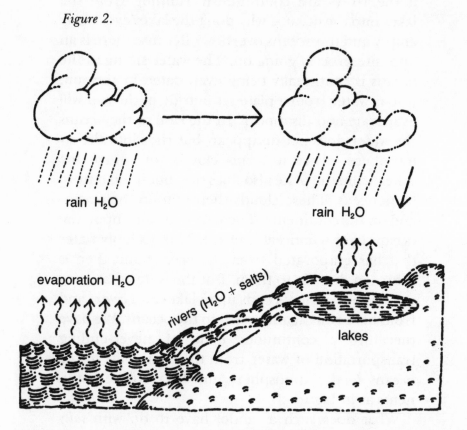

rain H₂O

rain H₂O

evaporation H₂O

rivers (H₂O + salts)

lakes

fore grow slowly but continuously more salty each year. And, in fact, precise experiments show that all this is indeed true, so this model of the *hydrologic cycle* does explain the salty oceans perfectly. (You could carry out the pertinent experiment yourself: simply dissolve some salt in a pan of water and let it sit in the sun. The water will evaporate in a day or so, and leave behind a coating of salt in the pan.)

In 1898 an Irish geologist, John Joly, carried the model one step further. He argued that if the rate of salt transported to the oceans has always been the same, and if the salt stays forever in the oceans, the process allows us to calculate how long it has taken for the oceans to become as salty as they have.

For example if we find that there is one pound of salt in all the oceans, and the rivers are bringing into the oceans one pound of salt per year, then we would calculate that the process must have started one year ago. This would be a ridiculous answer of course, but have no fear, there's a lot more salt than that in the oceans. In fact, Joly calculated that it would have taken eighty or ninety million years for all the oceans' salt to have been brought in by the rivers, and therefore that the earth was at least this old.

At about the same time Lord Kelvin, the outstanding British physicist of the day, presented another model. His was based on very simple and straightforward physics. He said that if the earth had been created together with the sun, or if it had been created somehow out of the sun, either way it must have been very hot at its birth; it must have been born as a molten ball of lava, at temperatures greater than 1,000°. Today its average temperature is about 20° (Centigrade of course—only idiots and Americans use Fahrenheit). Knowing the mass of the earth, he could calculate from the laws of physics how long it would take the earth to radiate away its heat and cool down to today's temperature. The result, he announced, was ten to twenty million years.

And this was a most interesting result, he went on, because of what it told us about the source of the sun's energy. If the earth (and the sun) were only a few thousand years old, then the sun might be just a normal earth-like fire. But such a fire could not possibly last several million years. *Gravitational energy*, however, could last that long.

By gravitational energy Kelvin meant the energy released by all the particles forming the sun as they fell in toward the center. In this model he visualized the sun as being formed from a cloud of particles which all fall in toward their mutual center; as they fall toward each other they form the sun and release gravitational energy. His calculations showed that such energy would be sufficient to produce the sun's light for millions of years, twenty or even thirty or forty million years.

But not for eighty or ninety million years. There simply wasn't enough gravitational energy in the sun to last that long. Therefore, he reasoned, Joly's estimate of the age of the earth must be wrong.

If there is not enough gravitational energy to last eighty million years, Joly countered, then there must be some other source of energy for the sun. For surely the earth (and therefore the sun) is at least this old, he insisted.

And so the geologists and the physicists lined up solidly against each other. The only thing they had in common was the certainty that the Bible was wrong.

Well, they had one other thing in common. They both were wrong.

Joly's model was correct as far as it went, but it was incomplete in assuming that the salt, once brought to the oceans, stayed there forever. It doesn't. There are wind effects which, surprisingly, blow salt from the surface of the oceans and return it to the land. If you stand on the shore you can *smell* the salt sea breezes. This means that it must have taken even *longer* than eighty or ninety million years to produce today's salty oceans.

Kelvin's model, on the other hand, had two errors. He didn't take into account the effect of *radioactivity*, which was being discovered at just about that time and which is a great source of energy. One of the most common forms of energy is heat, and so the existence of radioactive *atoms* in the earth means the existence in the earth of a source of heat unsuspected by Kelvin, and of course this upset all his calculations. A young physicist from New Zealand, Ernest Rutherford, showed that the earth's age might be as great as *billions* of years.

The other error in Kelvin's model was that it was *completely* wrong. We are pretty sure today that the earth did not start its existence as a molten ball of lava, but accumulated at a cold temperature and was subsequently heated up by its internal radioactivity. So the calculation about cooling down from a molten ball had absolutely nothing to recommend it except that, as modified by Rutherford, it turned out quite by accident to give an answer which is approximately correct.

The final solution to the problem came about during the next few years as Rutherford continued his experiments with radioactivity. In these experiments Rutherford and his students and coworkers discovered that one particular kind of radioactivity—alpha radioactivity—consists of a radioactive nucleus such as uranium throwing out an alpha particle. In fact the uranium goes through a succession of such alpha decays and ends up as an atom of lead.

Rutherford identified the alpha particle as the nucleus of a helium atom. He then realized that this discovery enabled him to measure the age of a rock directly. He worked out this idea in terms of the following model. Imagine a rock that is formed from lava cooling after it has been erupted from a volcano. The age of the rock will be the time since the volcanic eruption until today. There will be a small amount of uranium in the lava, as there is in everything on earth, even in you and me. The uranium will have been alpha-decaying continuously since the beginning of time, but all the helium formed *prior* to the eruption will bubble out and be lost when the hot molten lava erupts. The helium atoms produced after the lava cools into a rock, however, will be trapped and held in the crystal structure. As time goes on the amount of uranium will get smaller and the amount of helium will increase, as the uranium continues to decay. In other words, the ratio of helium to uranium within a rock will increase with time, or with the age of the rock. So if we can measure the helium and uranium in a rock, we can determine the age of that rock.

The rate at which any radioactive substance decays is measured by its half-life. This is the time that it takes for half of the radioactive substance to disintegrate. It is a well-known number for each radioactive substance and is constant throughout all time. For uranium-238, which is the main type of uranium found in rocks, the half-life is 4.5 billion years. This means that every four and one half billion years half of the uranium in the rock will have disintegrated, forming eight atoms of helium and one of lead (Figure 3).

Let's take an example. All rocks have a very small amount of uranium in them, usually about one millionth (0.000001 or 10^{-6}) of a gram in every gram of rock. Let's call this amount x. So if you picked up a typical rock like this soon after it was formed (not

Figure 3. The radioactive decay of uranium (^{238}U). Along the chain eight alpha particles (α) are emitted, which end up as helium atoms (^{4}He). Six beta particles (β) are also emitted; these are electrons and can be ignored.

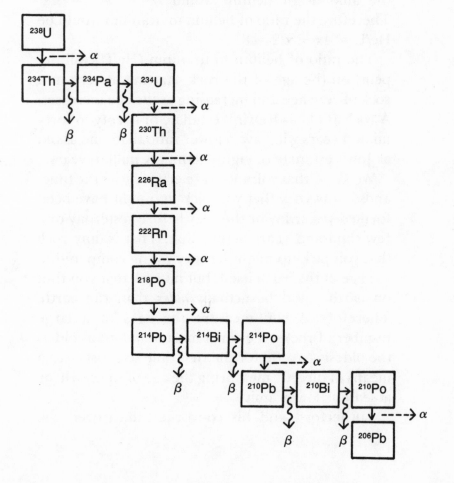

too soon after, because it is forming from molten lava and you don't want to burn your fingers), and if you measured the helium and uranium in it you would find x grams of uranium but no helium (U = x, and He = 0). Therefore the ratio of helium to uranium in this rock, a rock of zero age, would be He/U = 0/x = 0. If you waited four and one half billion years—one half-life—and then picked up the same rock and measured it again, you'd find that half of the uranium would have decayed. In this case the amount of uranium in each gram of rock would be one half the original amount ($\frac{x}{2}$) and the amount of helium would be $8 \cdot x/2 = 4x$. Therefore the ratio of helium to uranium would be He/U = 4x ÷ x/2 = 8.

The ratio of helium to uranium (He/U) will depend on the age of the rock, starting at zero in a rock of zero age and increasing as the age increases. A rock as old as Kelvin's estimate of twenty to forty million years will have a lower ratio than one as old as Joly's estimate of eighty to ninety million years.

We know that volcanoes are erupting all the time, and so any rock that you pick up might have been formed yesterday or the year before yesterday or a few thousand years before that. That is, any rock that you pick up might be very young compared to the age of the earth itself, but no rock that you find on earth could be actually *older* than the earth. Therefore if you measure the ages of a large number of rocks, the earth must be *at least* as old as the oldest rock. So for the first time scientists had a means of directly measuring the age of the earth, or at least its lower limit.

Rutherford and his co-workers measured the

uranium and helium contents of a great number of rocks and found that the ratio of helium to uranium turned out to indicate an age greater than Kelvin's estimate of the age of the earth, twenty to forty million years. It was also greater than Joly's estimate of eighty to ninety million years. The rocks turned out to be, in fact, *billions* of years old. And this of course meant that the earth must be at least this old, billions of years old!

Many refinements have since been carried out on this method of radioactive dating of rocks, and we know today that the earth is 4.6 billion years old. The sun, as we mentioned before, must be at least as old. We have said, remember, that the normal means of producing energy, by fires such as those we can produce on earth, would keep the sun hot for a few hundred or perhaps a few thousand years. And Lord Kelvin had shown that gravitational energy would keep it burning for millions of years. But neither source of energy could even come close to providing the necessary heat for *billions* of years. And so, for the ages determined by radioactive dating, a completely new source of energy was suddenly needed to explain the billion-years-old existence of the sun and the stars.

✿3✿
The
History of
Life

Not only did the great age of the earth mean that an entirely new form of energy was needed to provide the fuel for the sun, but the history of life on earth meant that this form of energy had to be of a very particular kind.

We know the history of life on earth through the records of our own race for the past few thousand years. But how do we know what happened before that? We can extend our knowledge another few thousand years by archeological studies, studying the remains of people who lived but left no written or oral records: studying the pottery they used and the buildings they built and the graves they dug. Probably the most ancient records of human life are the huge burial mounds or megalithic stone formations, such as Stonehenge in England. These actually tell us very little beyond the fact that there were people living at that time and place, and even so they extend our knowledge of life on earth back only to about six thousand years at most. If the earth is indeed four and one half billion years old then this six thousand years of history is a very

18

tiny portion of the total history of earth. How do we go back further? How do we learn the history of the life that existed before any records left by man?

We study the *fossil* remains of that life. A fossil is, by definition, anything that remains of a previous form of life. The shells you find on the beach are the fossils of animals which once lived in the sea and used those shells as homes and protection. The piece of coal you burn is the fossil remains of great swamps which teemed with life a hundred million years ago and were subsequently buried under the slow accumulation of sediments and transformed under the great pressure of burial through all the hundred million years of time into that lump of convenient coal. The gasoline that we use in our cars is another form of fossil buried by sediments.

Our world is full of fossils. We can dig down into the sand and mud at the bottom of the oceans and find shells of animals that lived millions of years ago and no longer exist on earth. We find buried in ancient forests and swamps the bones of dinosaurs that once roamed these lands. All over the world in different localities under different environmental conditions we find different kinds of fossils extending back to different periods of time into the past. Applying a series of forms of radioactive dating, similar to the dating of rocks with uranium and helium, we can measure the ages at which these animals were not fossils but living creatures. In this way, bone by bone, shell by shell, fossil by fossil, we extend our knowledge of previous life back millions, hundreds of millions, even billions of years.

The very earliest fossils are microscopic ones caught in rock fragments with ages of about three billion years. These are simple one-celled animals similar to the bacteria of today. We can follow the evolution of life in ever increasing forms of complexity from these simple forms through the fishes, the amphibians, the snakes, and the dinosaurs to the mammals and the rich diversity of species we see on earth today. In fact the richness of diversity produced by the evolutionary process is a bit too rich, isn't it? We could do today without some of the species with which we have to share the earth; not many of us would miss it if we lost all the mosquitoes, cockroaches, rats, and oil profiteers.

But never mind that, the important thing is that ever since the appearance of those first one-celled animals three billion years ago there has never been a period of time when the earth was without this continually evolving life. There was no period during which life was totally wiped off the face of the earth and had to begin again. This is a very important point when we consider the history of the sun, because life is based on the presence of liquid water. No life can exist without it, but liquid water is not stable under all conditions that exist everywhere in the universe. In fact, liquid water is stable under only a very limited range of temperatures. At $0°$ temperature it will change spontaneously into solid ice and at $100°$ it will change spontaneously into gaseous steam. Life cannot exist outside of this range of temperatures from $0°$ to $100°$.

Now what maintains the temperature on the surface of the earth? The sun, of course, the energy that is radiated from the surface of the sun to the surface of the earth. The surface of the sun is at a temperature of about $5,000°C$. The interior of the

sun is at a temperature of about 15,000,000°
$(15 \cdot 10^6)$. By the time this heat is radiated through
the vastness of space and reaches the surface of the
earth it is just sufficient to keep our earth at temperatures of between 20–25°. Now, imagine for
example that some sort of tidal wave existed in the
interior of the sun and brought some of that
15,000,000° central stuff out onto the surface of the
sun. Part of the surface would jump in temperature
from 5,000° to 15,000,000°. This would increase
the radiant energy so much that the temperature
on earth would jump by many hundreds of degrees. But water boils at 100°, and since we have an
uninterrupted procession of life on earth for the
past three billion years we can be absolutely certain
that nothing like this has ever happened; the sun
must have been burning at a very constant rate
without any great turnovers or fluctuations in temperatures. Because the temperature of the sun is
both so great and so different from surface to interior, any kind of a change in the sun would reflect
itself in a large temperature variation on earth. It
would very quickly take the earth's temperature
above 100°, and the continuous history of life on
earth says that nothing like this ever happened.

So we not only need an energy source for the sun
that is sufficient to keep the sun burning for at least
four and one half billion years, we need a source of
energy that will burn at a very precise and constant
rate for at least the past three billion years. Such a
constancy of energy production is a very unusual
thing; it could not be accidental. For example, if
you watch a fire burning in the fireplace, or a house
on fire, or any fire burning under natural condi-

tions, you'll notice that it occasionally flares up, occasionally dies down, is hotter at the beginning and cooler later on, and in general burns at a pretty irregular rate. The only fires that burn at a constant rate are those which are controlled, for example the fire when you turn on your stove. Such a fire must have an internal control to keep it going at the desired rate; so it must be with the sun. The source of energy that burns the sun must be internally controlled. The mechanism which controls it must somehow be precisely set so that it burns at exactly the same rate and gives off precisely the same amount of heat for at least the past three billion years.

Now, if you were God, how would you work out a mechanism like that?

✵4✵
Little
Green Elves,
or Whatever

When Lord Kelvin predicted that the earth was "only" twenty to forty million years old, he had shown that the only source of solar energy that could last that long was gravitational. If it should ever be shown that the sun was older than that, he warned, it would necessitate a new, mysterious, previously unsuspected kind of energy. Now suddenly the earth, and therefore the sun, was indeed shown to be much older than that. Further, this mysterious new kind of solar energy was necessarily under careful control, keeping the earth's surface temperature at about 20° for billions of years.

Whenever some such precise control is found in nature, some people are quick to jump up and shout, "See! That proves there must be a God!"

Well, perhaps. And perhaps it "proves" that there are little green elves living in the sun who check the temperature three times a day. Or perhaps we can find a purely physical, non-supernatural process that controls the sun. At least, before falling back on little green elves or gods or whatever, let's give it a try.

In fact, at just about the same time that the need for a new, mysterious, previously unsuspected kind of energy became known, a discovery was being made by other scientists of —guess what?

A new, mysterious, previously unsuspected kind of energy!

✿5✿
$E = mc^2$, etc.

In 1905, when formulating his theory of relativity, Einstein had derived the equation $E=mc^2$. This says that energy (E) and mass (m) are related; they are, in fact, only different forms of the same stuff, which he called *mass-energy*.

If this were really true, he continued, it should be possible to convert one form into the other. The equation tells us what the result of such a transformation would be: the amount of energy obtainable from a piece of mass is equal to that mass multiplied by an extremely large number (c^2). c is the *velocity* of light, and if we use the metric system, where the mass is measured in grams, the velocity of light is 3×10^{10} centimeters per second, or 30,000,000,000 centimeters per second. The value of c^2 is then 9×10^{20} or 900,000,000,000,000,000,000. This means that if even one gram of matter were to be converted into energy the amount of energy generated would be mc^2 or $1 \times 9 \times 10^{20}$ gram-centimeters squared per second squared, which is an enormous amount of energy. It's enough to break iron chains or stop a speeding locomotive or even lift it up over tall buildings at a single bound. It's about a million times more energy than we get from the normal processes of burning things. For example if you could convert the tip of a match entirely into energy, the resulting flash would not only light a cigarette but would light you and your house and most of the city lying around it.

But all Einstein's theory told us was that it was possible to liberate this much energy from ordinary matter; he didn't tell us how to go about doing it.

Nobody had the faintest idea how to go about doing it, until it was realized that this is in fact what is happening in the processes of radioactive decay which were being studied by Rutherford. When an atom of uranium-238 decays it forms eight atoms of helium and one of lead-206. When the atoms of uranium, lead, and helium were weighed very accurately—as they could be with a new instrument called the mass spectrometer—a very interesting fact was found. The lead and the helium, when added together, did not weigh as much as the original uranium. The precise numbers that were measured turned out to be that uranium-238 weighed 238.1252, the lead-206 weighed 206.0388, and each helium atom weighed 4.0039. Together the lead and helium weighed $206.0388 + 8 \times 4.0039 = 238.0700$, less than the 238.1252 weight of the original uranium.

What happened to the missing mass? Before Einstein we had always believed that mass could never be created or destroyed, only changed from one form to another. Here was a case, however, where mass seemed to disappear completely. Einstein's equation, $E = mc^2$, told us that what had happened was that the missing mass had been converted into energy; it is in fact this nuclear mass-energy which provides the awesome and terrible energy associated with nuclear reactions and the atomic bomb.

Could this awesome and terrible energy somehow be the source of the sun's fire? Well, yes and no, to be perfectly frank.

In order to explain that answer, in order to understand how the mass of atoms can be converted into energy, we'll first have to learn something about what atoms actually look like.

✶6✶

The Structure of Atoms

All of the universe is composed of the same kinds of atoms. There are no mysterious elements such as Kryptonite to be found on distant planets; the sun and the stars and the planets and the moon and the earth are all composed of the same elements, although different elements may be more or less abundant in these different places.

The number of elements is not unlimited. There are only eighty-three different kinds of *stable atoms* in the whole universe. By stable we mean atoms which will remain the same forever unless subjected to outside change. Up until this century it was always thought that *all* atoms were stable, that nothing could ever change them. But we now know that the process of radioactivity is in fact the spontaneous change of one kind of atom into another, and with our nuclear reactors and atom smashers we can ourselves change any of the stable atoms into others by bombarding them with nuclear projectiles.

Aside from the stable elements, there are about two dozen radioactive elements. Some of these, such as uranium and thorium, occur naturally on earth, while others exist only for short periods of time when they are created in our laboratories. In addition there is the possibility of some super-heavy elements that may at one time have existed but no longer do.

The question you should ask at this point is, how do we know? How do we know that there is not some mysterious element that has not yet been discovered? How do we know that when we go to Jupiter or Saturn we won't find it composed of entirely different elements than we have here on earth?

That's a very good question. I'm glad you asked it. The answer is that the differences between different kinds of atoms are not mysterious differences; they are a definite pattern which changes in a step-by-step fashion from one atom to another, and there are no holes in this pattern. There is simply no place where a new and mysterious element could fit in.

The way to understand this is simply to take a look at the pattern, which is a very simple one indeed.

All atoms are composed of three particles: *neutrons*, *protons*, and *electrons*. The neutrons and the protons fit together in the *nucleus* of the atom, with the electrons spinning around outside. The atom thus looks like a miniature solar system, with the nucleus playing the part of the sun and the electrons the part of the planets (Figure 4). The important characteristics of these particles are their *mass* (or their weight) and their electrical *charge*. Both the neutron and the proton have about the same mass (about 1 on an atomic scale), while the elec-

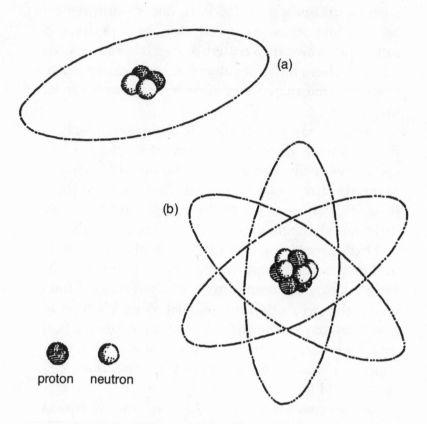

Figure 4. In (a) we have a ^{4}He atom, with two protons and two neutrons in the nucleus, and two electrons going around it in the one orbit shown. If there are more than two electrons, as in the heavier atom shown in (b), there must be more electronic orbits. The electrons, themselves, are so small that on this scale they cannot be seen.

tron has negligible mass (about zero). The electrical charge of the proton is $+1$ and of the electron -1, while the neutron has zero charge.

These three particles are put together to make atoms so that the number of protons is approximately equal to the number of neutrons and the number of protons is *exactly* equal to the number of electrons. When two atoms come together to form a chemical reaction, such as when paper unites with oxygen to form a fire, the electrons of one atom touch and interact with the electrons of the other. But the nuclei of the two atoms never touch and never react. Therefore it is the number of electrons in each atom that determines what its chemical behavior will be. Since it is by means of this chemical behavior that we define what we call the elements, it follows that if two atoms have identical numbers of electrons they are by definition atoms of the *same* element. And if two atoms have different numbers of electrons they must be atoms of *different* elements. The simplest way to understand this is to start at the beginning and see how all the atoms are constructed, beginning with the simplest atom.

The simplest atom we can conceive of would be an atom with just one particle in its nucleus. This can be either a proton or a neutron. If it is a neutron then the number of electrons (which must equal the number of protons, which in this case is zero) must be zero, and so we have simply a neutron sitting by itself. A neutron all by itself is radioactive and will change spontaneously into a proton plus an electron within a few minutes, so we won't consider this case any longer.

The other simplest possible atom is an atom with just one *proton* in its nucleus. Since the number of protons is approximately equal to the number of neutrons, the number of neutrons may be either zero, one, or two. The simplest case, of course, is if it is zero; in this case we have a nucleus consisting of only one proton, and since the number of electrons must equal the number of protons we have one electron circling around it. This atom is given the name *hydrogen*. Starting with this simplest example, we can construct all the other atoms by adding more and more atomic particles: protons, neutrons, and electrons. Let's see what happens when we do.

If we add a neutron to this hydrogen atom the number of electrons will remain the same. Since the number of electrons is the same, this new atom will behave chemically in a manner identical to that of hydrogen. It therefore is *still* an atom of hydrogen. Since its nucleus is different, it is called a different *isotope* of hydrogen. The simplest isotope of hydrogen has a mass equal to one (because of its single proton); this slightly more complicated isotope has a mass of two, because of its proton plus neutron. We therefore call the simplest isotope hydrogen-1 or ^1H and the heavier isotope hydrogen-2 or ^2H.

If we add another neutron to this atom we will form another isotope of hydrogen called hydrogen-3 or ^3H. If we try to add another neutron we find that the new isotope, hydrogen-4, cannot exist because now the numbers of neutrons and protons are becoming too dissimilar and the atom will break down. So there are just these three possible isotopes of hydrogen, the simplest possible element.

Instead of adding neutrons to hydrogen what happens if we add protons? If we add a proton to hydrogen-1 the resulting atom cannot exist, because of the great dissimilarity in the numbers of protons and neutrons (two protons and zero neutrons). But we can add a proton to hydrogen-2. This will give us a new atom with two protons and one neutron in the nucleus. Since we have added a proton we must also add an electron, because the number of protons and electrons *must* be identical. Since we have added an electron, the new atom will not be chemically identical to hydrogen and therefore it forms an atom of a new element: this element has been called *helium* and the resulting atom is therefore helium-3, or ^{3}He.

We cannot form another new atom by adding a third proton, because then the number of protons and neutrons would again be too dissimilar (three protons and only one neutron). But we *can* add another neutron. In this case we have formed a new isotope of helium, helium-4 (^{4}He).

In this manner, adding one proton or neutron at a time, we can describe all the atoms in the universe and all their isotopes. Figure 5 shows a chart which describes the most common isotopes of the light elements. This chart can be continued, forming new elements simply by adding a new proton (with of course a new electron each time) until we have created all the elements that exist.

Eventually, as we add new protons and neutrons, the atoms will get so big that they are no longer stable. That happens when we reach eighty-three protons, the element bismuth. If we add more protons than this the resulting atom cannot be stable and must *always* be radioactive. Atoms with fewer protons than this may or may not be radioactive, depending on how similar their number of protons and neutrons are. As the numbers get more and more dissimilar the atoms are more likely to be radioactive; but above this number of protons the

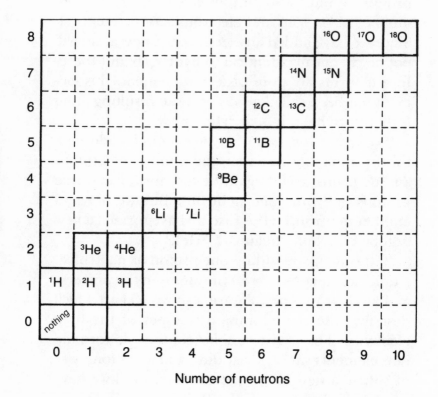

Figure 5. A chart of the light elements. The "element" with zero protons and zero neutrons is, of course, nothing. With zero protons and one neutron we have only a neutron. With one proton we have the three isotopes of hydrogen; with two protons we have the two isotopes of helium, then lithium, beryllium, etc.

atoms *must* be radioactive and cannot be stable. In this manner we know exactly what elements are possible in this universe.

Now what does all this have to do with the problem of producing enormous amounts of energy in stars?

☼7☼

More
About
Atoms

Well, not much. But I'm coming to that. You will
recall the exhilaration with which we discovered a
mysterious new form of energy in Chapter Five.
This exhilaration was shared by everyone at the
time of the original discoveries of radioactivity. In
fact, even before Einstein had explained the source
of nuclear energy—as the result of the conversion
of mass into energy—there had been speculation
that here might be, somehow, the source of the
sun's light. The simplest explanation, offered as far
back as the year 1898 by an English gentleman-
astronomer, was that the sun might be composed in
large part of a radioactive element such as radium
or uranium. If so, the radioactive decay, which we
know in the case of uranium will go on for billions
of years, might certainly provide the necessary
energy.

This was a good idea and it got people thinking
in the right direction, but it turned out to be wrong
as an explanation of the sun's energy, for two reasons.

The first reason has to do with the concept of

half-life which we discussed before. The half-life of uranium-238 is 4.5 billion years. That means four and one half billion years ago there was twice as much uranium in the sun as there is today. This means that the energy produced at that time, and therefore the temperature of the sun if this is indeed the energy source of the sun, was twice as great then as it is today. Three billion years ago the energy would have been nearly twice as great, the temperature nearly twice as high. This means that the temperature on earth would have been well over 100° three billion years ago, and no life could have existed at that time. Since we know there *was* life at that time, this is obviously an impossible situation.

The second reason is that there simply is not enough uranium in the sun to provide the necessary amount of energy. How do we know how much uranium is in the sun? You wouldn't believe me if I told you, not at this stage. We first have to learn a bit more about the *quantum mechanical* structure of atoms. So let's get on with it.

The hydrogen atom, you remember, consists of one proton in the nucleus and one electron whirling around it. At about the same time that Einstein was formulating his theory of relativity a Danish physicist named Niels Bohr explained the structure of the hydrogen atom on the basis of a new *quantum theory*. He worked out that the electron must whirl around the nucleus not just in any old orbit but in a very precise location. It could not vary from atom to atom or as time goes by; the electron must be always at a very precise distance from the nucleus.

And once he had established this, he wondered what might happen if you heat up the atom.

If you heat something you are putting energy into it. This means that the atom must be absorbing the energy. Where does the hydrogen atom store this energy that it is absorbing? Well, if it is absorbing energy something must happen to it. But what? After worrying and wondering and working for a long time, he finally came to the conclusion that what happens is that the electron is pushed farther out from the nucleus. But it doesn't just wander out a little bit at a time as it absorbs the energy bit by bit. Instead, nothing happens until a certain small but finite amount of energy is added to the atom, and then the electron jumps to a larger orbit. This is known as a "quantum jump." If more energy is added, again the atom can do nothing about it until another finite amount is received and then the electron will jump out to a farther precisely defined orbit. The possible orbits for the electron in a hydrogen atom are shown in Figure 6.

Only one of these orbits, the innermost one marked by the *quantum number* n = 1, is a stable orbit. This means that all hydrogen atoms under normal conditions will have their electrons in that orbit. But when energy is added to the atom, as when the atom is heated, then the electron may jump to any one of the other allowed orbits depending on the amount of energy added. Of course since there is only one electron in a hydrogen atom, only one of these orbits will be occupied in any one atom at any particular time. Since all of the orbits except n = 1 are unstable, when an atom is pushed

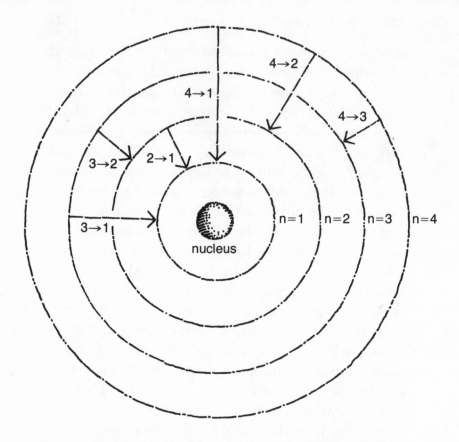

Figure 6. Sketch showing the quantum jumps from the excited states n = 2, 3, 4 to the normal state n = 1.

into one of them it will immediately jump back down to the n = 1 orbit. When this is done, an amount of energy is released corresponding exactly to the energy difference between the orbits.

For example, if a hydrogen atom is heated so that its electron pops up into the n = 2 orbit it will then immediately drop back into n = 1 and a flash of light with energy precisely equal to the difference between the n = 1 and n = 2 orbits will be given off. Now light of different energies is identified by its different wave lengths. We can build machines called *optical spectrometers* which can measure the different wave lengths in a beam of light. The light that we normally see on earth is composed of a mixture of all different wave lengths. In fact this is what gives light its different colors to our eyes; red light has a different wave length than green light, for example. If we were to look at a group of hydrogen atoms which had all been excited to the $n = 2$ state and which then emitted light corresponding to the $n = 2 \rightarrow n = 1$ quantum jump we would instead see only light of one particular wave length. (To our eyes there would be nothing special about this light, but the optical spectrometer would tell us that it consists of only this one particular wave length.)

In general, if a large number of hydrogen atoms are heated the electrons will pop into all the different possible quantum states and will then all fly hippity-hop (or higgledy-piggledy) back to the $n = 1$ state. If the source of heat is continuous, they will be reheated right back to the various quantum states and will then continue to emit light as they drop back into the $n = 1$ state and are reheated as this process continues on and on. If we look with the optical spectrometer at this hot mass of hydrogen atoms we will see a mixture of wave lengths, but they will not be simply any old wave lengths. They will be a mixture of just those particular wave lengths which are allowed by the transitions $n = 2 \rightarrow n = 1$, plus $n = 3 \rightarrow n = 2$, plus $n = 3 \rightarrow n = 1$, etc. We will see wave lengths of certain definite values, only these and no others.

Now don't forget we said that the particular orbits that characterize hydrogen atoms are the same for all *hydrogen* atoms, but they are different for all different *kinds* of atoms. This means that if we were to look at a bunch of *helium* atoms being heated up the process would be the same; the electrons around the helium nucleus would be in their normal form at a certain quantum state n = 1 and as they were heated they would pop up to different quantum states n = 2, n = 3, and so on. But the location of these various quantum states would be *different* for the helium atom than for the hydrogen atom, and therefore the transition between any two states (for example n = 2→n = 1) in helium would give a burst of light with different energy and therefore a different wave length than the transition between the same states in the hydrogen atom. This means that if we look with an optical spectrometer at a mass of hot helium we will again see light consisting of a number of discrete wave lengths, but these wave lengths will be *different* from those we see coming from the hydrogen gas. Therefore the optical spectrometer can tell us whether the gas we are looking at consists of hydrogen or helium.

In fact every atom has its characteristic electron orbits and therefore emits light of characteristic wave lengths. By looking at the light emitted from hot atoms we can tell precisely what kind of atoms are emitting the light.

The application to the sun and stars is obvious then, isn't it? All we have to do is look at them with an optical spectrometer and measure the wave lengths of the light coming out of them. This will tell us precisely what kind of atoms the sun and stars are made of. This type of research is known as optical spectroscopy. When we do this, we find that the wave lengths which characterize uranium atoms are not seen. This tells us that the sun is not composed of uranium. Nor is it composed of radium, nor of any other radioactive element.

Instead, we find that the sun—and all the stars, for they are remarkably similar—is composed nearly entirely of the simplest possible atoms: hydrogen and helium.

✸8✸
A Sort of
a Problem

Actually, this looked at first like a very serious problem. I mean, constructing a sun out of hydrogen and helium? You'd have to be out of your mind.

Why? Well, look around you. Here on earth there's hydrogen everywhere—you can't get away from the stuff. Our oceans and rivers and rain and 99% of our Coca-Cola are H_2O, molecules composed of two atoms of hydrogen and one of oxygen. And all that water doesn't look much like turning into a solar-type fire. It's true that hydrogen can burn with oxygen under the right conditions, but that was just the kind of fire that physicists like Lord Kelvin had shown couldn't keep the sun going for more than a few thousand years. For a 4.5-billion-year-old sun it was no help at all.

And helium is even worse. Helium is one of the "noble gases," and like nobility these gases do no work at all. It was known that they wouldn't burn under *any* conditions. So how are you going to make the sun and stars burn for billions of years with only hydrogen and helium?

The answer, though strictly speaking having

nothing to do with radioactive atoms, was found in basically the same kind of studies that led to the source of the nuclear energy. Let's think of the atoms in terms of a progression from the simplest to the more complicated.

The simplest possible atom is hydrogen, with one proton and one electron. We said in Chapter Six that both the neutron and the proton have a mass of 1, while the electron's mass is essentially zero. Then the total hydrogen atom should have a mass of 1, while a helium atom should have a mass of 4.

A helium atom, in fact, can be thought of as 4 hydrogen atoms squeezed together to form a new atom. If this were done you would end up with an atom of four protons and no neutrons. This would certainly not be stable and two of the protons would spontaneously change into neutrons, giving an atom of two protons and two neutrons—an atom of helium-4.

But when the masses of the hydrogen and helium atoms were measured precisely in the mass spectrometer, it was discovered that the hydrogen atom actually weighs slightly more than 1; its mass is 1.0082. Four of them would therefore have a mass of 4.0328. The helium atom actually weighs slightly *less* than this; its mass is 4.0039. Therefore if four hydrogen atoms are squeezed together to form one helium atom, we have started with a mass of 4.0328 and we end up with a mass of only 4.0039. Some of the mass has disappeared.

Well, the people doing the experiment looked around the laboratory, under the benches, in their pockets, and even in their coffee cups, but they could not find that missing mass. And then they remembered what Einstein had been telling them—that $E = mc^2$.

What happens in the formation of the helium atom from the four hydrogen atoms is that the missing mass is converted into energy. And although the amount of mass that disappears is very very small, the energy that it becomes is that mass multiplied by c^2, which becomes a very large number indeed. So potentially the conversion of hydrogen into helium is a source of *tremendous* energy. It turns out to be even more than the energy from the radioactive decay of uranium. Taken together with the observed fact that the sun is composed mostly of hydrogen, we have here a process that could provide *millions* of times more energy than if the sun were burning some conventional fuel. If a body the size of the sun, burning with conventional fuel, could last a few thousand years, then if it could get its energy from converting hydrogen into helium it could last millions of times longer—and millions times thousands is billions ($10^6 \times 10^3 = 10^9$). A star or sun burning in this manner could last easily the 4.5 billion years that was needed to satisfy our knowledge of the age of the earth.

Wow! They thought they had something here. But it wasn't all quite so simple; there were other problems involved. For example, how about the known fact that the temperature of the sun must have been very constant for the last three billion years. How could the conversion of hydrogen into helium provide such a *constant* fire? In fact, although theoretically it's a lovely process, how does it actually occur? What gets it started, what turns it on? And doesn't this lead to another problem? If the spontaneous conversion of hydrogen into helium provides the sun's fire, why doesn't the same thing happen here on earth? Why doesn't the hydrogen on earth turn on, and turn us all into a flaming star? Help!

A Star
Is Born

The problem we're talking about lies in the fact that there is lots of hydrogen on earth as well as in the sun. All our oceans and lakes and clouds and toilet bowls are full of water, and water is H_2O. These water molecules are the result of the normal kind of chemical reaction in which the electrons of hydrogen merge with the electrons of oxygen to form a stable molecule. The structure of the molecule can be visualized as in Figure 7. In other words, although the electrons of hydrogen and oxygen react with each other, their nuclei never touch.

But why not? If in the sun the nuclei of hydrogen atoms fuse together to form helium, why doesn't the same thing happen here on earth?

Well, it's a good thing it doesn't, right? Think of the air-conditioning bills if the surface temperature of the earth were 5,000°. To see what prevents it, let's look at the structure of the hydrogen atom. We said a few chapters ago that all atoms are neutral because the number of negatively charged electrons is always identical to the number of positively charged protons. But the *nuclei* of atoms are not

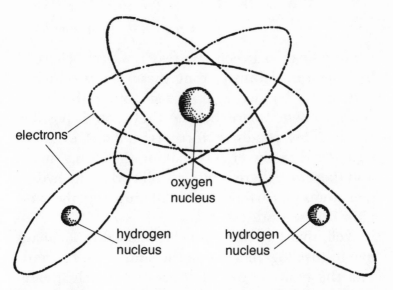

Figure 7. Structure of the H_2O molecule. The electrons of hydrogen and oxygen interact to hold the molecule together, while the nuclei remain aloof.

neutral, since there are no electrons in the nucleus. The nucleus of every atom, consisting only of protons and neutrons, is always positively charged. When two positively charged particles approach each other there is an electric *repulsive force* between them which will try to keep them apart. This is a general consequence of the nature of electrical charge; *like* charges repel and *opposite* charges attract each other. A similar effect can be seen when playing with magnets; the opposite ends of bar magnets will attract each other strongly but the like ends will repel each other just as strongly.

In our world all atoms are constantly in motion; heat is a form of energy that makes atoms shake. Therefore all the hydrogen atoms in all the water molecules in all the waters of earth are constantly vibrating, and in doing so they are constantly bouncing against each other. But the electrical repulsive force between the two positively charged hydrogen nuclei is so strong that when two hydrogen atoms bounce against each other this force pushes them apart before they could possibly touch. This repulsive force is millions of times stronger than the energy making the atoms shake, and therefore there is no possibility that the hydrogen atoms on earth will naturally fuse together and blow up the world.

Well, that's a relief. But then how do they manage to fuse together inside the sun? Well, for starters, the temperature of the sun is much greater than that on earth. As temperature rises so does the vibration of the atoms caused by the heat-energy. At the tremendous temperature at the center of the sun (about 15,000,000°, remember) the atoms are shaking so violently that when two hydrogen atoms collide they do so with such force that they crash right through the electric repulsive barrier and fuse together.

Well, you may say, that sounds all right, but how did the sun get that hot to start with? If the fusion of hydrogen provides the heat for the sun and if the heat of the sun is necessary to cause the fusion of hydrogen, how did it all start? Which came first, the chicken or the egg? And how about that old problem of keeping the energy supply constant? Remember the sun has to burn at precisely the same rate for billions of years. How does the fusion of hydrogen accomplish this? Why doesn't all the hydrogen just fuse together into helium and cause one big brilliant explosion, leaving a dead sun behind?

To understand all this, let's think about how the

sun, and the stars, must have formed. At one time there must have been no sun, no stars. Then what was there?

We think that the empty reaches of space, between the stars today and before the stars when there were no stars, is not and was not quite empty. It is filled instead with minute particles of gas and dust. This is the raw material out of which the universe is made. Throughout eons of empty time this gas and dust swirl aimlessly throughout the not-quite-empty universe. Eventually a large number of these gas and dust particles happen to come fairly close together. We are not sure precisely what mechanism causes them to do this; probably the easiest way to think of it is simply to think about what will happen if all these gas and dust particles are just moving at random in the universe forever. Eventually, just by chance, a large number of them will end up in the same region of space. When this happens the mutual forces of gravity between the particles begin to attract each other.

Now gravity is a very interesting natural force. Every particle that exists in the universe possesses an intrinsic force of gravity which will try to attract every other particle to it. But it is a very weak force. For example, you yourself exert a force of gravity on everything around you, including other people. But the force is so very weak that almost nobody feels attracted to you. At least nobody feels very attracted to me. There is an attractive force of gravity between every two hydrogen atoms pulling them together, but this force is billions and billions of times weaker than the repulsive electrical force pushing them apart, and so the force of gravity between two hydrogen atoms will never cause them to fuse together.

But the interesting thing about gravity is that its effects add on to each other. That is, in Figure 8, atom A exerts its gravity on atom B and vice versa. This does not stop atoms A and B from each exerting an equal force of gravity on atom C and vice

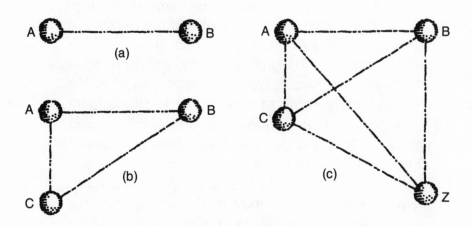

Figure 8. In (a) we have two atoms A and B exerting a gravitational force on each other. Addition of a third atom C in (b) does not change the force between A and B, nor does addition of a fourth atom Z in (c) although the force between Z and the others is less because the distance is greater.

versa. In fact every atom in a given group exerts its full force of gravity on each and every other atom within that group. The only thing that can diminish that force of gravity is distance; the force of gravity drops off very rapidly with distance, so that the force of gravity between atoms A and B is much greater than that between atoms A and Z. But the total amount of gravitational energy among any group of particles is proportional to the total number of particles: if there is a certain amount of gravitational energy existing between two atoms A and B that are a certain distance from each other, and if you could then crowd in ten atoms within that same distance, the total amount of gravity would be the same between each pair of ten atoms so that the total amount of gravity would be 10 × 9/2 = 45 times the original (let's see you figure that one out!). In other words as you put more and more atoms into a certain space the amount of *total* gravitational attraction between them increases. And if you put the same number of atoms into a progressively smaller space, again the amount of gravitational attraction will continually increase (Figure 9).

Figure 9. There is a certain gravitational attraction (indicated by the arrows) between every atom in group (a) and every other atom. In group (b) the attraction between each of the atoms is increased because they are closer together.

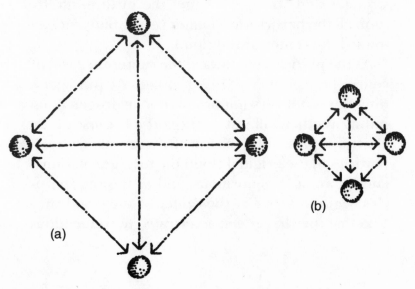

(a)

(b)

Now, keeping these ideas in mind, think of a cloud of dust and gas particles out there in space. It is possible that each particle might be so far away from every other particle that the forces of gravitational attraction between them would be very small. In such a case there would be nothing to hold the cloud together and all the particles would eventually drift away from each other. On the other hand it is also possible that there might be enough particles close enough together that the sum total of their gravitational attractions would be the dominant force acting between them. And in this case the cloud of particles would stay together as a cohesive unit. In fact the particles would now all begin to fall toward each other, pulled by their mutual gravity, and as the particles get closer together the gravitational attraction between them gets even stronger (remember Figure 9?) so the particles now begin to fall together even faster. As they do, the gravity between them continues to get stronger and stronger, which makes them fall faster and faster so they get closer and closer so the gravity gets stronger and stronger . . . get the picture? Pretty soon all the particles are falling very rapidly indeed toward the center of the cloud.

As the particles fall toward the center they will of course be banging into each other. At the beginning this is not very important; one hydrogen atom hitting another will just bounce off it because of the electric repulsive force. But if there were enough particles in the original cloud the total gravitational energy would be enormous, and as the first particles begin to arrive at the center of the cloud they find that they have been accelerated to tremendous velocities. These atoms are now moving so fast that they have energies a million times greater than the energies involved in normal chemical reactions; in fact, they have enough energy to overcome the repulsive force that two hydrogen nuclei exert upon each other. In this situation, if two hydrogen atoms collide they will fuse together. When four such hydrogen atoms fuse together in this fashion they will form an atom of helium and the mass difference will be released as energy.

What happens now? We have a cloud of gas and dust that is being pulled together by its own gravitational attraction. All the atoms are being sucked in toward the center. Those reaching the center have acquired very great velocities and as they smash into each other they fuse together and form helium, thus producing energy. This energy now radiates outward, providing light and heat and acting *against* the inward-sucking force of gravity.

The light and heat provided by this nuclear energy mean that the cloud of gas and dust up there in the sky now begins to glow. It is giving off light and heat, shining in the darkness, and looks like a star. In fact, it *is* a star. As the energy radiates outward, it counteracts the gravitational energy pulling the particles inward and the whole mass achieves a state of balance. If the inward gravitational energy becomes greater than the outward radiant energy the particles of the star will fall in toward the center, but as they do they acquire more velocity and more of them will fuse together to form helium, releasing more radiant energy until the radiant energy again comes into balance with the gravitational energy. If the radiant energy, on the other hand, becomes too great, then particles instead of falling into the star will begin to drift out away from it. This will slow down the nuclear reactions taking place at the center, decreasing the outward flow of radiant energy until once again it is balanced by the gravitational energy. In this way the outward energy (nuclear radiant) and the inward energy (gravity) *always* remain in a state of balance, and the star will sit up there in the sky continuing to burn at precisely the same rate while the hydrogen in the center is being converted into helium.

The details of the process, as you can imagine, are very complicated. But it is possible to calculate the rate at which it proceeds, and the results of the calculations indicate that a star the size of the sun will burn in this manner at a constant rate for somewhere around ten billion years. So this model of a star is perfectly satisfactory to account for the facts that the sun is four and a half billion years old, and that it has been burning at the same rate for at least the past two or three billion years. And it gives us another five billion years of sunlight, which is very nice for Miami Beach.

✪ 10 ✪

Problems,
Problems,
Problems...

So now we have a model of the sun and stars which says that they gain their energy by fusing hydrogen into helium. This predicts that the sun and stars should be composed mostly of hydrogen with a little helium, and when we look at them with optical spectrometers we see that this is precisely so. Furthermore, we calculate that this source of energy should last for several billions of years and this is precisely the time needed in view of the age of 4.6 billion years for the earth. Finally the nuclear energy of the stars is triggered by the gravitational energy in just such a way as to keep the engine running at a very constant rate throughout the lifetime of the star, which we had known was a necessary feature from the presence of life on earth over the past three billion years.

So this model of stars looks like a very good model, and we can begin now to ask it a few further questions. For example, eventually a star will use up all its hydrogen. There will be no further source of energy. What happens then? In other words, this model tells us how stars live: by fusing hydrogen

55

for their energy. Can the model also tell us how stars die?

And there is another problem that may have occurred to you. We've seen that this model predicts that stars should be composed of hydrogen and helium, and indeed they are. But we, you and I, are not. We are composed of several different elements: in addition to hydrogen we are mostly carbon, nitrogen, and oxygen. These are much more complicated elements. Carbon has six protons, six neutrons, and six electrons; nitrogen has seven protons, seven neutrons, and seven electrons, while oxygen has eight of each. If the universe started out as pure hydrogen, the simplest possible element (as seems most reasonable), and if this hydrogen is converted to helium inside stars, and if that is the end of the story, then where did all the nitrogen, carbon, and oxygen come from to make our bodies?

And the problem gets even worse than that. The earth we live on is composed mostly of oxygen, silicon, and iron. Silicon has fourteen protons, neutrons, and electrons, while iron has twenty-six protons and thirty neutrons. In addition, when we measure the materials of the earth very accurately we find that every rock contains at least minute amounts of every single one of the elements, from hydrogen all the way up to uranium! In fact, so do our bodies.

These other, more complicated, elements are obviously of great importance to us; we wouldn't exist without them. And yet our model of the stars does not even mention them. Now *that*, you have to admit, is a problem.

✡ II ✡

Normal Stars
and Not So
Normal Stars

According to our model all stars should be pretty much the same. They form from a cloud of gas and dust which is mostly hydrogen and they burn by fusing the hydrogen into helium. If this is true of all stars, then how different can one be from another? So the question then arises, *are* all stars the same?

But what does this question mean? What·do we mean by "the same"? By sameness we only mean sameness in those qualities of the stars that we can measure. So what is it that we can measure about the stars? We know that we can look at the wave lengths of the light coming out of the stars and from them tell what chemicals the stars are made of. Is there anything else we can measure?

The answer must obviously be yes, or I wouldn't have mentioned it. So think of your stove. Why? Never mind, just think of it. In fact, go look at it. In fact, turn it on (careful!). If it's a gas stove you should be able to notice that the flames coming out of it seem to be yellowish at the center with a blue envelope rising above the yellow. Why this differ-

ence in color? It's because the flame is actually
burning at different temperatures. The yellowish
spot at the center is the lowest temperature and the
blue envelope rising above it is the same gas burning at a higher temperature. The difference in
temperature results in a difference in color. If your
stove is an electric one, you will see that when it is
turned on the black coils begin to glow red. Now
think of movies or television shows you have seen
which show molten iron being poured from vats in
a factory. That stuff is glowing white. The difference in color between the cold black iron coils and
the glowing red iron coils and the molten white iron
in the factory is again a difference of temperature.
When an object is heated it begins first to glow dull
red, then as the temperature increases the color
changes to an orange-yellow and to blue and then
finally to white.

Our sun is a yellowish star. If all stars are at the
same temperature they would all be yellowish. On
the other hand if they are burning at different
temperatures they should exhibit a difference in
colors. When we look at a star with our naked eye
all we can see is a pinpoint of light; our eyes are not
sensitive enough to distinguish various colors from
such a small point of light. But it is possible to make
instruments which can record precisely the colors
of the light.

It is also possible to make instruments that will
measure the total energy emitted by the sun. If
another star were the same size and burning at the
same temperature it would certainly emit the same
amount of energy. But a bigger star will emit more
energy, a smaller star less.

It is therefore possible to look at the stars and determine their color (which tells us their surface temperature) and the total energy they emit (which tells us what size they are).

If all stars are precisely like the sun, the same size burning at the same temperature, then they would all look identical in these measurements. But according to our model we would not expect this. If each star forms from a condensing cloud of gas and dust, there is no reason to expect each of these condensing clouds to be exactly the same size. Therefore we should end up with stars of different sizes. A larger star will have more gravitational energy pulling it together and therefore will fuse hydrogen at a faster rate in its center, and therefore will burn at a higher temperature. So we expect, when we look at the stars, to see stars with a wide range of masses and a correspondingly wide range of temperatures. But if the nuclear processes which provide their energy are the same for each of these stars then the variation in masses and temperature should be related. They should give a smooth curve when plotted on a graph. When this is done we find that indeed most of the stars do lie along such a smooth curve. This is shown in Figure 10.

This diagram is called the Hertzsprung-Russell diagram, after the two astronomers who first thought of using the data in this manner. The larger stars lie toward the top of this diagram and the very brightest stars lie toward the left. Most of the stars that we observe lie on the smooth curve rising from the lower right-hand corner to the upper left-hand corner. This is called the Main Sequence. It makes perfect sense according to our

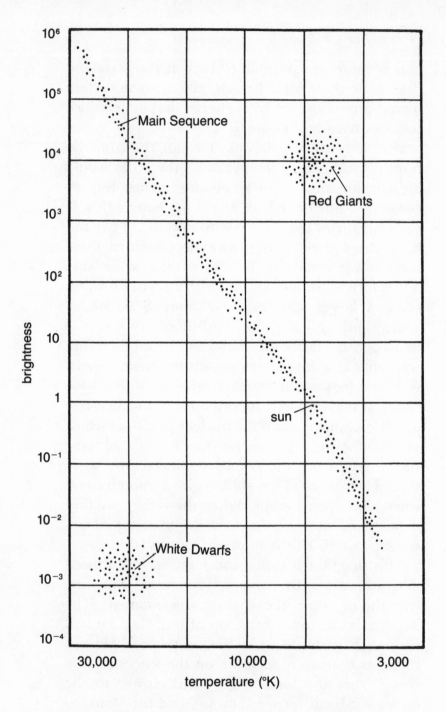

Figure 10. The Hertzsprung-Russell diagram.

model because, starting for example from where the sun is located, if a star is bigger than the sun it should be higher than it on the diagram but it should also be burning at a hotter temperature and therefore be to the left of it; if it is both higher than it and to the left of it, that means it is displaced along the curve toward the upper left-hand corner. On the other hand if a star is smaller than the sun it should lie below it, but it should also be burning at a less hot temperature and therefore should lie along the curve toward the lower right-hand corner. Therefore the model fits most of the data.

But it doesn't fit *all* of the data, does it? In particular there are two groups of stars which do not lie along the Main Sequence and therefore must have different sources of energy. In the upper right-hand corner there is a group of stars much bigger than the sun, but also much cooler. Their low temperatures are indicated by a reddish color, whereas their high emission of energy indicates that they are giant stars. These giant reddish stars are called, naturally enough, *Red Giants*.

There is another group of stars much smaller than the sun but burning with a white color, meaning that they are much hotter. These small white stars are called *White Dwarfs*.

Our model of stars must be modified to take into account the Red Giants and White Dwarfs, and to explain them. What next?

✿ 12 ✿

The Life
and Death of
Stars

We already knew we were going to modify and extend the model, didn't we? Because the model of stars that we have mentioned so far explains how they are born and how they live for billions of years, fusing their hydrogen into helium. But billions of years, although rather a long time, isn't forever, is it? And so we know that eventually they must use up all their hydrogen, and must die. Certainly when they do so, they're going to change their appearance. But our model so far hasn't told us how. What we have to do now is follow our model through to the end to see if along the way it will explain the Red Giants and White Dwarfs, and the very complicated atoms of which you and I are composed. It is only if it fails to explain these observations when carried through to its ultimate conclusion that we will have to begin to worry about the model.

So then, what happens when a star uses up all its hydrogen fuel? Remember that the star began as a vast collection of hydrogen atoms all falling toward the center of the cloud because of their mutual gravitational attraction. As they fell closer into the center the gravitational energy became greater and they fell faster and faster, until finally they were colliding together at high enough velocities that they could penetrate the repulsive barrier and fuse together into helium. When this happened they began to generate nuclear energy, which balanced the gravitational energy and left the star in a stable state, fusing hydrogen into helium and producing energy that could continue for billions of years. In this state the star takes its position on the main sequence, depending on its mass (stars larger than the sun lying upward and to the left of it, stars smaller than the sun lying below it and to its right).

As time goes on the hydrogen in the center of the star is gradually being transformed into helium. Eventually ths star will end up having a core which is more helium than hydrogen (Figure 11). The fusion of hydrogen to helium can only take place at the center of the star, since only there is the gravitational pressure sufficient to overcome the repulsive barrier. So when the star reaches the situation illustrated in Figure 11, where its core is depleted in hydrogen, the fusion process slows down and stops.

Why can it not continue with hydrogen fusing with the already formed helium? Two reasons. First, each helium nucleus has two protons and therefore a positive charge twice as great as that of the hydrogen. This means that the repulsive force between the helium nucleus and a hydrogen nucleus will be twice as repulsive as that between two hydrogen nuclei, and this will be enough to prevent their fusing together. But second, even if they could overcome this repulsive barrier, what would

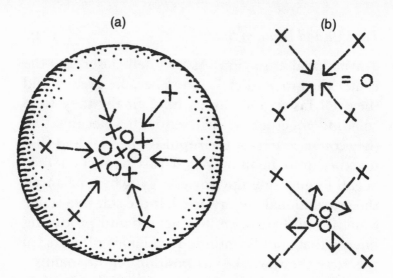

Figure 11. In (a) we see a star's gravity pulling the hydrogen (x's) toward the center of the star, where they fuse into helium (o's). The helium buildup at the center dilutes the hydrogen, and the effect is shown in (b); where no helium is present, the hydrogens fuse together to form helium. But if helium atoms are already there, the hydrogen will bounce off them, slowing down and eventually stopping the process.

happen? The fusion of a hydrogen nucleus (one proton) with a helium nucleus (two protons and two neutrons) would result in a new nucleus with three protons and two neutrons, and if you will look at Figure 5 you will see that such a nucleus simply does not exist. And so the process cannot take place, and the colliding hydrogen and helium will just bounce off each other and go their separate ways.

From the time the star first turned on until now it has been in a stable situation, with the gravitational energy which pulls all the particles toward the center precisely balanced by the nuclear energy which flows out from the center. Now suddenly, as the fusion process dies down, there is no more nuclear energy flowing out. What happens?

Very clearly the gravitational energy is going to take over. Once more the particles will start falling in toward the center. As they do, the gravitational energy will increase and the core of the star will get hotter and hotter. The helium atoms in the core will be smashing against each other furiously, hitting each other harder and harder as the temperature in the core increases. Now what result, do you think, is this going to have?

Certainly two helium nuclei can't fuse together, because the repulsive barrier between the two doubly charged nuclei is *four* times as great as that between two hydrogen nuclei, right? (H: $1 \times 1 = 1$. He: $2 \times 2 = 4$.) But as the star now collapses inward and it becomes more compressed and the gravitational energy increases and the core gets hotter and hotter, eventually the helium atoms are falling together with *so* much speed and *so* much energy that when they collide the impact is sufficient to overcome even this high a repulsive barrier. And indeed they *can* fuse together.

What, do you think, happens now?

This question had been studied for many years and the answer, rather disappointingly, seemed to be that nothing very much at all would happen. The atom resulting from such a fusion would have a mass of eight (four protons and four neutrons) and, again consulting Figure 5, this atom also does not exist. It is so unstable that it immediately splits back apart into the two helium atoms.

But in the early 1950s Edwin Salpeter, an Austrian-American physicist at Cornell University, made some very interesting calculations which showed the possibility that *three* helium nuclei might fuse together to form the stable nucleus of the carbon-12 atom. Experiments were subsequently carried out at Cal Tech which showed that this reaction could actually take place under the proper conditions. When this happens the star's core will again begin to release energy because the carbon-12 atom weighs a little bit less than the three helium atoms, and therefore in this process once again nuclear mass is converted into nuclear energy.

We now reach a new state of thermal equilibrium with nuclear energy once again flowing out of the core of the star and balancing the gravitational energy flowing in. But what does this new form of the star look like? Well, for one thing it will be smaller because it has collapsed, right?

Well, uh, no. It will actually be *bigger* than it was. You see, when the star stopped fusing hydrogen and collapsed, the core got very much hotter than it had been. The core of our own sun (which is a typical hydrogen-fusing star on the Main Sequence) is burning at about 15,000,000°. The core of a similar star that has collapsed and has started to fuse helium into carbon will be burning at a temperature of about 100,000,000°. When a gas such as hydrogen or helium gets hotter it exerts more and more pressure. You could test this by blowing up a balloon and then putting the balloon in the refrigerator. As it cools off in the refrigerator the pressure of the gas inside will become less and the balloon will shrink. On the other hand, if you put it out in the hot sun where the gas inside can be gently warmed the pressure will increase and the size of the balloon will swell. This is precisely what happens to our collapsed star. When the interior becomes hotter the star swells and grows. It therefore becomes not a dwarf star, but a giant; in the Hertzsprung-Russell diagram (Figure 10) it moves up.

Now what about its color? Will it move to the left or to the right in the diagram? Well, its temperature in the center is much higher, therefore it should move to the left. Right?

Sorry. Wrong again. When we look at a star we cannot see all the way into the center because the star is too dense. We actually see only the surface of the star, which is being heated by the nuclear fire going on in the center. But the surface itself is at a much lower temperature than the center because it is very far away from it. Remember we said that the interior of the sun is at about 15,000,000° but its surface temperature is only about 5,000°. Obviously the temperature of an object is cooler the farther away it is from whatever fire is heating it. You can test this principle easily by holding your hand near a match, then moving it closer and closer to the match. You can feel the heat getting hotter and hotter as you get closer and closer until—ouch! Dammit.

Well, it's the same thing in a star. The surface of a star on the Main Sequence is at a certain temperature because it is at a certain distance from the interior nuclear fire. When the hydrogen fuel is all consumed and the star collapses nothing much happens until a new nuclear fuel is generated at the center by the fusion of helium into carbon. This now becomes *so* hot that the star expands and the outside surface of the star is pushed much farther away from the center than it had been. The sun, for example, when it becomes a Red Giant will expand to about one hundred times its present size. So even though the core of the star gets hotter than it had been when it was on the Main Sequence, the surface of the giant star is now so far away from this central fire that the surface becomes *cooler*. As it becomes cooler, it changes color from a nice luminous orange, as in the sun, to a dull red. On the Hertzsprung-Russell diagram this moves it to the right.

And what do we have? We have a Red Giant. How about that?

Now what about the White Dwarfs? Can our model explain them also? Well, our star isn't dead yet. Let's continue the story of what happens to it during its lifetime, and let's see what happens.

As time continues to go on, more and more helium is converted to carbon and so the core of the star becomes progressively enriched in carbon and depleted in helium. The nuclear energy is provided by the fusion of the helium atoms; the presence of the carbon atoms adds nothing to this nuclear energy. In fact, the carbon serves only to dilute the helium fuel (just as the growing presence of helium diluted the hydrogen fuel in the Main Sequence stage). As the carbon builds up and the helium becomes more and more diluted the nuclear energy furnace becomes less and less efficient. Less and less helium is fused together and the nuclear energy begins to die down. Eventually it must stop.

From this point onward, the direction of the star's evolution depends on its size. For a star about the size of the sun, the future is relatively simple.

The nuclear furnace in the core turns off and the diluted envelope around it becomes unstable and is blown off into space. The core, meanwhile, has no longer any outward radiant energy to resist the tug of gravity and so falls in upon itself, contracting until its atoms are squeezed in upon themselves nearly as tightly as passengers in a New York bus on a rainy afternoon at rush hour. The point is finally reached at which no more passengers can be squeezed into the bus and at which the atoms can be squeezed no more tightly into the core, and there they all sit forever—the passengers waiting for the traffic to move and the atoms waiting for eternity (which is the same thing).

What do they look like? The atoms, I mean; forget the passengers (as the Metropolitan Transit Authority seems to have done). The core has collapsed as far as it can so it will be a small star, a dwarf star. And during its compression it will be heated white-hot. So what do we have?

A White Dwarf. Bingo.

We even have direct proof that all this actually occurs because we have seen it happening. There are objects in the sky called *planetary nebulae*, in which the Red Giant envelopes are actually seen in the process of blowing away, and at the center of them we see a White Dwarf remaining behind (Figure 12).

The model leads naturally to this last group of observed stars, the White Dwarfs, as the dying corpses of once normal stars. These White Dwarfs have no nuclear energy left to burn. They are white-hot from the energy of the gravitational collapse, but are producing no more energy of their

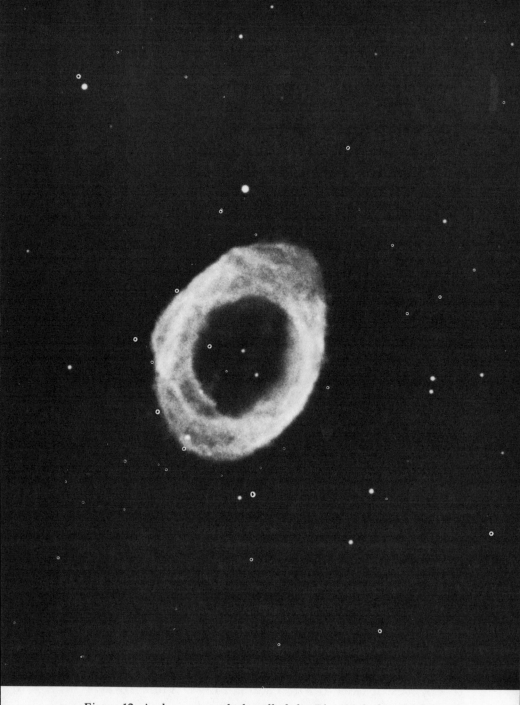

Figure 12. A planetary nebula called the Ring Nebula, which is the remnant of a red giant star blowing away its envelope. (*Lick Observatory Photographs*)

own. In time they fade away into invisible Black Dwarfs and litter the heavens like invisible beer cans on a public beach. Wouldn't it be nice if all those beer cans were also invisible?

So there we are. Our model has successfully described all these astronomical objects and explained what makes them tick: normal stars, Red Giants, and White Dwarfs, with planetary nebulae and sweating, cursing bus passengers thrown in *en passant* (look it up).

But is that enough?

You'd think the astronomers and astrophysicists would be satisfied with that, wouldn't you? But no, as soon as they get a model that explains all the observations they go on and ask the model what else it *predicts*. Can the model not only explain what we see, but also tell us what else to look for? After all our thousands of years of looking up at the stars, can this model predict the existence of things up there we have not yet seen?

Can it?

Well . . .

✳ 13 ✳

Something New
Beyond the Sun

... actually, yes.

In the last chapter we said that a star like the sun ends its Red Giant stage when the helium in the core is exhausted. But there are stars in the sky ten times, or even a hundred times, the size of the sun. For these massive stars, evolution beyond the Red Giant phase follows a different sequence of events, and ends in a different death.

If the star is five to ten times the mass of the sun, the contraction of the core (following the end of the helium fuel) is driven by correspondingly greater gravitational energy. In this case the core is heated to about 600,000,000° and this temperature is hot enough to fuse carbon nuclei together ($^{12}C + ^{12}C \rightarrow ^{24}Mg$). This releases more energy and the temperature rises still further, increasing the rate of carbon fusion, which in turn raises the temperature still further so that everything begins to fuse ($^{12}C + ^{4}He \rightarrow ^{16}O$, $^{12}C + ^{24}Mg \rightarrow ^{36}Ar$, etc.) and the nuclear reaction quickly runs out of control.

What do you call a nuclear reaction that has run out of control? You call it an atomic explosion, and that's exactly what happens to this star. The whole thing explodes in one tremendous blast that can be seen throughout the entire galaxy.

It dwarfs any H-bomb explosion set up on earth or the most terrible magnetic storms ever to exist on the sun or even the sudden roar of applause when Julius Erving steals the basketball and dunks it. It is called a *supernova* (from the Latin words *nova*, meaning new, and *super*, meaning super) and happens in our galaxy about once every few hundred years. It's now been about five hundred years since the last supernova, so one is due any night now. Go take a look, maybe tonight you'll be lucky.

What will you see when the next supernova goes off? What you will see is a star in the sky that you never noticed before because it was just one of the innumerable and ordinary stars in the sky. But tonight it will be different, tonight it will be a very bright shining star. Tomorrow might when you go looking for it you won't miss it; it will be even brighter. Night after night, for a few days or weeks, it will grow and grow until it is the brightest star in the sky, perhaps giving off as much light as the full moon. It might even be visible in daylight. Then it will slowly begin to dim and night after night it will grow dimmer and dimmer until, after a month or two, it will fade out of sight and be gone.

It will be gone to the naked eye, but not to our telescopes. If you look at the fading supernova through a telescope you will see that as its light grows dimmer it gets larger and larger. What you are actually seeing now is the expanding cloud of gas and dust that has exploded from the surface of the star and is spreading out to be lost into space.

Is all this for real? It certainly is. How do we know? Well, in the year A.D. 1054 there is a record in the Chinese histories of a new star suddenly appearing in the sky. This star grew brighter and brighter for a few weeks, then faded away and disappeared. At its brightest it was the brightest star in the sky, nearly as bright as the full moon. The rest of us weren't nearly quite so civilized then as the Chinese, but wherever there are writings of that period a bright new star is mentioned, and where there are no writings there are pictures scratched on cave walls of a crescent moon and a bright star next to it. From the Chinese records it has been possible to pinpoint precisely where in the sky the new star was, and when we look at that point in the sky today through a good telescope we see what is shown in Figure 13. This is the Crab Nebula, an expanding cloud of gas and dust which is the remnant of the supernova of A.D. 1054. It is still expanding today, still dispersing, and someday will be lost as each of its particles fades away into the universe.

And is that the end of the supernova? Not quite. For as in a normal star, here too it is only the outer portion of the star that is blown away, the core instead being *compressed* by the explosion. The force of this compression is so great that the atoms are smashed together and their structure is actually destroyed. Remember Figure 4? Well, in the core of the supernova the atoms are squeezed together with such force that the electrons are squeezed right into the nucleus! There they merge with the protons to form neutrons, so the entire core of the star now has no atoms at all but is composed solely

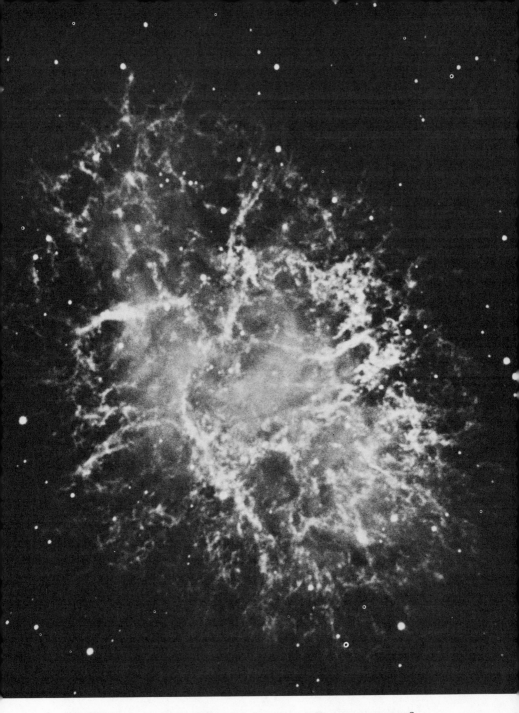

Figure 13. The Crab Nebula, the expanding remnant of a supernova explosion that was seen in 1054 A.D. (*Lick Observatory Photographs*)

of neutrons. And we have named it, subtly enough, a *neutron star*.

It was easy enough to name it, but what next? How do we prove it exists? What do we look for? Who knows what a neutron star is supposed to look like anyway? Here we have a case of the model predicting something we had never dreamed might exist and therefore we can't imagine what it might look like.

And it gets worse. We said that other stars are as large as one hundred times the sun, and these *very* massive stars follow a still different evolutionary path. In these stars the nuclear fusion process continues, because of exceedingly high temperatures, all the way up to iron-56, with twenty-six protons and thirty neutrons. And at this point something new happens.

Up till this point, every time two or three nuclei fused together to form a new one, the new one weighed less than the sum of the original ones and the resulting missing mass then showed up as energy. But now it all changes. The reaction $4 \, ^1H \rightarrow ^4He$ gave more energy than $3 \, ^4He \rightarrow ^{12}C$, which in turn gave more energy than $^4He + ^{12}C \rightarrow ^{16}O$, etc. In other words, each succeeding fusion reaction gave less energy than the one before it. Now, finally, with the formation of the iron-group nuclei, we run out of energy. These nuclei have the most efficient mass-energy ratios, so fusing them with other nuclei will not provide any more energy. If we try, for example, to fuse iron with carbon the resulting mass *increases*, so instead of liberating energy it would soak it up. The massive star has been too greedy for energy and has fused itself into catastrophe (a lesson for all stars, planets, or countries too greedy for energy).

At this point the nuclear energy radiating out from the core must stop, and so the star begins to collapse. This time there is nothing to stop it; no further source of nuclear energy exists. On the contrary, as the core collapses the iron nuclei are smashed around and begin to break up into helium, carbon, oxygen—into any atom of mass less than fifty-six. And the transformation of iron into those atoms *absorbs* energy. So the core collapses even faster, and so still more iron nuclei break up, absorbing even more energy, and the core collapses faster and faster and—woof!

Woof is the antonym of *bang* and signifies the opposite of an explosion, an *implosion*. The core implodes inward with increasing speed as the shattering iron nuclei suck up gravitational energy faster than it is released; the outer layers of the star, with the core sucked out from underneath, also fall inward. As the core momentarily forms a neutron star, the outer layers come crashing in on it. Temperatures flash up past a *billion* degrees, and the outer layers explode into a supernova.

But what happens to the imploded core? The velocities of the atoms at this stage are so high, approaching the speed of light, and the gravitational pressure so intense, that we have to turn to Einstein's theory of relativity to find out what's happening.

Early in this century, Einstein had calculated that if it were ever possible to throw atoms together quickly enough so that the gravitational pressure rose high enough, a state of infinite space-time curvature might result.

"Infinite space-time curvature, eh," scientists mumbled to themselves as they read his papers. "What could that mean?"

A good question. For many years it was thought that it didn't mean much of anything at all, since nowhere in our universe could the impossibly great gravitational conditions be reached. But as more detailed calculations on the collapse of massive stars were carried out, it was realized that in these stellar cores such gravitation would in fact be encountered. So all right, then, what *does* infinite space-time curvature mean?

✪14✪

Black
Holes

Einstein's theory of relativity interprets the universe as being composed of a space-time continuum, rather than of separate space and time. All this really means is that in setting up equations with which to calculate certain physical effects, time must be treated as nothing much more than a fourth spatial coordinate (in addition to length, breadth, and height).

Science-fiction writers and comic strip cartoonists soon picked up this idea and transformed it into a mysterious "fourth dimension" through which their heroes travel to different universes to encounter weird villains in exotic settings. In actual truth this "fourth dimension"—time—is not at all mysterious, but when merged with space in the manner described by Einstein, it leads us to a different concept of a universe where we do indeed encounter weird objects in the most exotic of settings. To understand all this, we begin with the most common of all forces, gravity.

Gravity is treated in relativity theory as a curvature in the space-time continuum. What does that mean? Consider an ordinary two-dimensional space, such as the top of a table, and imagine a ball rolling across it. If the table is not tilted and is perfectly smooth, the ball will roll straight across it without swerving.

But suppose the tabletop is made of a piece of cheap wood which has warped. Then instead of rolling in a straight line, the ball will curve according to the warped surface.

This is equivalent to the relativistic description of gravity. Gravity is a curvature or warp in the space-time continuum in which the universe exists, and anything moving in such a gravitational field must curve along with this curvature. So if you throw a ball up into the air, it curves around and falls down again. In the absence of any gravity (curvature) it would simply go on flying in a straight line forever.

The strength of gravity at the surface of an object depends on the object's mass and size. This means that the more a star is compressed, the stronger the gravity at its surface (Figure 14); in relativistic words, the greater the curvature of space-time that surrounds it. Back in 1915, shortly after Einstein gave this description of gravity, a German colleague of his named Karl Schwarzschild wondered what would happen if a star began to shrink. As it grew smaller, he reasoned, the gravitational warping of space-time around it would get more intense. This increase in gravity would squeeze it still smaller, which would further intensify the gravity surrounding it, which would make it still smaller, and so on and on until—what?

Until it would vanish, was Schwarzschild's amaz-

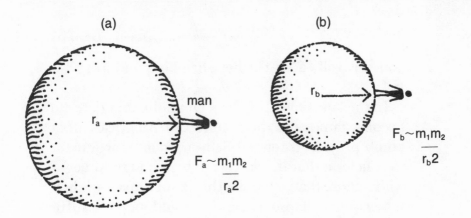

(a)   (b)

man

r_a ——→●

$F_a \sim \dfrac{m_1 m_2}{r_a{}^2}$

r_b ——→

$F_b \sim \dfrac{m_1 m_2}{r_b{}^2}$

Figure 14. Here we have two stars of the *same mass*: star (b) is compressed to a smaller size than star (a). The force of gravity that a man would feel at the surface of each star depends on his mass (m_1) and the star's mass (m_2) and the distance to the center of the star (r). Since r_b is smaller than r_a, the force of gravity (F_b) exerted by star (b) on the man is greater than that (F_a) exerted by star (a).

ing answer. The star would literally squeeze itself to death, and beyond death to nothingness.

This seemed a bit fantastic, even nonsensical. Nobody worried very much about it, however, because after all how could such a preposterous catastrophe happen in the first place? Schwarzschild's whole line of reasoning began with the presumption that a star might *begin to shrink*. And could such a thing happen? It was like arguing about the number of angels that could dance on a pin.

But now, suddenly, with our increased insight into the physical processes taking place inside stars, we saw in the last chapter that the core of a star might actually *implode*. Certainly this is a reasonable way to begin the Schwarzschild process of stellar shrinking. In other words, once the core begins to implode the gravity surrounding it will increase and this will cause further shrinking and away we go!

In the late 1930s J. Robert Oppenheimer (later to become famous as the architect of America's atom bomb project) extended Schwarzschild's argument to conclude that if a star were big enough to begin with—more than ten times the size of the sun—when it began to collapse its gravity would increase sufficiently to do just what Schwarzschild had said: the gravity would increase and the star would grow smaller and on and on *without limit*. This means that nothing could slow or stop the process, and so the gravity would increase to *infinity* and the star would shrink until it *disappeared*.

How can that happen? Well, you're not going to believe me, but think of it like this. You're standing here on the surface of the earth and you throw a ball up and it falls down. If you threw it hard enough, it would break loose from the earth's gravity, right? In fact, we can do this, not with a baseball but with a rocket. Great. Now if the gravity around earth were increasing, it would take more and more energy to throw a rocket free of it. Eventually, when the gravity increased to infinity, it would become impossible. There is not enough energy in the whole universe to break through an infinite field of gravity.

In fact, when the gravity becomes infinite *nothing* can escape. If you were to fly a spaceship onto the surface of an imploding star with infinite gravity and then stand there and shine a flashlight up into the sky, the beam of light would bend over and fall back down! Light itself cannot escape infinite gravity! (Of course, if you were stupid enough to try this experiment you'd never get away with it. Your body would be crushed by the force of gravity long before your spaceship got anywhere near the imploding star.)

So what we have, and what Einstein's relativity and our model predict, is the imploding core of a massive star with an infinite curvature of space-time around its surface. The temperature of this star is billions of degrees, much hotter than our sun, but no one can see it! It is *invisible*.

It is invisible because, in order for an object to be seen, it must emit or reflect light from its surface to the eye of the observer. For example, you see a blade of grass when it reflects sunlight (or the light from your flashlight at night) back to you. You see the sun because it emits light. But a star that is surrounded by an *infinite* gravitational curvature of space-time can emit no light at all, no matter how hot or bright it actually is. Because, as we said, nothing can break through an infinite field of gravity. Nothing, not rockets or spaceships or Superman or even a beam of light. The light that it would normally emit is trapped by the gravity, bent around so tightly that it falls right back down on itself. Neither light nor anything else can escape the surface of this object, and so it must remain invisible to the outside world.

You couldn't see it by shining a light on it from outside, either, because any such outside light reaching it would also be curved around so tightly that it could never get away again. Any light—and anything else, spaceships and little green elves and radio waves, anything!—that ventures into this infinitely curved space is trapped there forever. And so the theoretical collapsing star was named a black hole, after the infamous escape-proof prison in Calcutta.

Again, as with the neutron star, easy enough to name it, but how do you find one? What would a black hole look like?

It would look like what it sounds like, a black hole, a nothing. Since we see objects by seeing the light emitted from them or reflected by them, and since a black hole emits and reflects *nothing*, it would be invisible against the blackness of space.

And so, many years went by, and no one saw a neutron star or a black hole. And then, one stormy black night on the haunted moors of England, a radio star began to wink at a pretty girl in distress . . .

✪15✪

Pulsars
and
Black Swans

Jocelyn Bell was the pretty girl, a graduate student in astronomy at the university in Cambridge, and she was in distress because nobody believed her when she said that she saw what she saw when she saw it. She had built her own telescope to look at radio waves from the stars, and when she looked she saw—

But first you have to understand that radio waves are different from light waves only in their wave length, and stars that emit their energy at these wave lengths are called *radio stars*. They are observed by gigantic antenna systems called *radio telescopes*, and in 1967 Jo Bell was engaged in just this kind of research. She was making a survey of faint radio stars, looking for behavior similar to the "twinkling" of normal stars, when she noticed that one particular radio star was giving off short bursts of energy very rapidly and very regularly. The bursts were incredibly short, lasting less than one hundredth of a second, and were repeated at precise intervals of 1.3373013 seconds.

Reporting this odd behavior, she was told to

check it again since it was impossible. It was impossible for two reasons. First, when an object emits energy it is spread out and received on earth at different times due to the size of the emitting object, blurring the precision of the signal and spreading out its length. The smaller the object, the less the blurring and spreading. Jo Bell and her fellow workers soon calculated that signals received in bursts of less than one hundredth of a second duration indicated an emitting object that was less than ten miles in radius. The sun is nearly a half-million miles in radius; the smallest known stars, the White Dwarfs, are about ten thousands miles in radius. *Ten miles?* Impossible!

Second, the regularity of the bursts, one every 1.3373013 seconds, was more precise than any natural astronomical process was known to be, or thought possible to be. The whole thing was utterly absurd.

So back she went to the lab, but every time she looked, again and again, there was that same star winking at her, each wink lasting less than one hundredth of a second and coming precisely every 1.3373013 seconds.

The scientists at Cambridge began to think that she was receiving signals from an *extraterrestrial* civilization. They could think of no other way to explain the small size of the emitting object—a satellite? a spaceship?—and the regularity of the bursts. They referred to the signals among themselves as LGMs, using the classic science-fiction term for alien beings, Little Green Men.

And then Miss Bell discovered another LGM, and then another. Other workers, looking more

Jocelyn Bell   Tom Gold

carefully now, found still others. Suddenly the sky
seemed to be full of these winking wonders. The
great number of them argued against the LGM
theory; there might certainly be another civilization
out there calling to us, but never so many of them,
and all calling in just the same way.

The answer to this intriguing problem of the *pulsars* (as they were now called) came from Professor
Tom Gold, already one of the most famous astronomers in the world, at Cornell University. He
suggested that the pulsars are actually the neutron
stars whose existence had been predicted by our
model of stellar evolution. The extremely dense,
imploded state of neutron matter would explain
the small size of the pulsars, with the core of a massive star squeezed into a ten mile radius. The
characteristic pulsating emission of radiation was
tougher to explain, but he managed it.

He pointed out that a neutron star would be expected to have a particularly intense magnetic field and that as a result of its collapse it should be spinning rapidly. The effect of the magnetic field would be to focus its outgoing radiation at a single point on its surface; as a result of its spinning, this spot would swirl around and send out a beam of radiation just as a rotating lighthouse beacon does (Figure 15.) We would see it only when it came around and pointed directly at us, and then we would see it as a wink, a blink, a pulse of energy.

Experimental confirmation of this view came quickly when a pulsar was found at the center of the Crab Nebula. If the Crab is the remnant of the supernova of A.D. 1054 then according to our model there must be a neutron star left behind at its center. People had looked for it before, but not knowing what a neutron star might look like, they

Figure 15. The radiation emitted by a neutron star is constrained by its intense magnetic field. As the star spins, a lighthouse effect is produced.

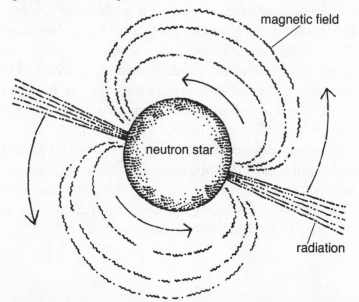

had found nothing. Now that they knew what to look for, suddenly there it was (Figure 16)!

The discovery of the first black hole by comparison seems nearly prosaic. A few years later, in 1970, NASA sent up satellite Uhuru to look for X-rays coming from outer space. And Uhuru found them, coming from an object called Cyg X-1 in the constellation Cygnus (The Swan). The X-ray source was pulsating, and its periodicity required an object smaller than a White Dwarf.

Figure 16. In the very center of the Crab Nebula is a neutron star, which we see as a pulsar. These two consecutive photographs show the pulsar beamed toward us (the brightest spot in the bottom photo) and away from us (invisible in the top photo). (*Lick Observatory Photographs*)

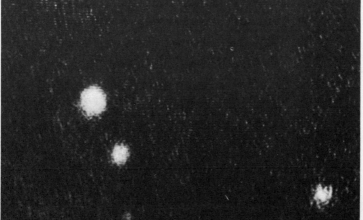

Perhaps a neutron star? But there was no evidence in Cyg X-1 of a supernova, and the mass of the source turned out to be much greater than that calculated for neutron stars. In visible light Cyg X-1 was identified as a binary star with an invisible twin; that is, when we looked at it we saw what appears to be a normal star orbiting around *nothing*. Many binary star systems are known, consisting of two stars orbiting around each other. But a star orbiting around nothing at all is impossible, so clearly there is something else there—something that is invisible.

And the X-rays? Where do they come from? The best explanation we have is that illustrated in Figure 17, where a black hole is sucking material from

Figure 17. Material is being sucked from the visible star in Cygnus X-1 and is spiraling inward and disappearing into the invisible black hole. As it disappears, X-rays are given off. The visible companion star to the black hole is orbiting around it.

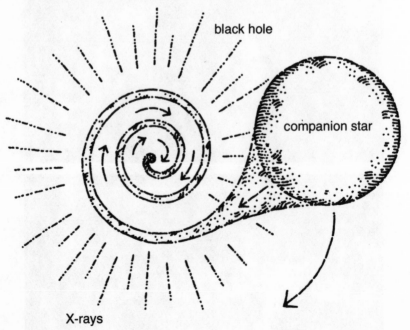

black hole

companion star

X-rays

its companion star. As the material spirals inward it is heated to millions of degrees just before it disappears forever into the hole, and it is well known that such a hot gas will emit energy, some of it in the form of X-rays.

All in all, the only explanation for a star orbiting around "nothing," where the "nothing" has a mass greater than the sun and emits X-rays, is a black hole. If the actual existence of such black holes is confirmed by future work, the possibilities seem endless. Many theorists are now betting, for example, that the black holes will explain the mystery of the *quasars*.

Quasars, or QSOs, or quasi-stellar objects, are not-quite stars that shine with the energy of a hundred *billion* stars. The mystery arises from the fact that none of the nuclear energy sources we have been discussing in this book are capable of providing one star-like object with so much energy. The solution (or the *possible* solution) arises from the fact that when a black hole sucks objects into it and in doing so emits energy (as in the Black Swan Cygnus X-1), it can convert as much as 10% of the doomed mass into energy. Nuclear fusion, lighting up the stars, is nowhere near as efficient, converting only about 0.1% of the mass into energy.

So the black hole model of quasars consists of a gigantic black hole, formed by a mass of maybe a million or even several billion suns, sitting in the center of a galaxy and eating that galaxy, devouring it, sucking it in a whole star at a gulp and swallowing it whole and in the process spewing out 10% of the star-food as quasar energy. In fact, the eventual end of all galaxies, including our own, may be to disappear down the gullet of a black hole.

What actually happens to stars sucked into a black hole? Nobody knows. Inside a black hole we are in a region of space-time with infinite curvature, and here all our notions of the laws of physics disappear. In other words, no one knows, in fact, if there is anything at all inside a black hole!

One interpretation of Einstein's theory is that at conditions of infinite space-time curvature the material that formed the black hole has crushed itself out of existence, it has compressed itself to an infinitesimally small volume, it has shrunk to *nothing*. If that is true, then the inside of a black hole is actually empty. It began as an enormous mass sucking in on itself, and ends as a region of infinitely curved but empty space-time!

And what of the material that formed it? Where is it now? *"Geh' weiss,"* Einstein might have said, "Who knows?" Some claim it has ceased to exist, others argue that it may have been spewed out in another universe or another dimension, whatever *that* means. Some science-fiction writers talk about using black holes as tunnels to go from one place to another beyond the speed of light, but there's a lot more fiction than science in such nonsense, since in entering the black hole anyone would be crushed out of existence once and for all. If he is spat out again elsewhere he certainly won't be in the same form and he certainly won't be still alive.

Even without such science-fiction scenarios, black holes are exciting things—or non-things—to think about. Stephen Hawking, a theoretician at Cambridge University, has carried the intricate relationships between quantum mechanics and relativity to a point where the equations predict that mini black holes should have been created at the moment of the creation of the universe in a Big Bang. These tiny black holes are the size of an atom and were created when planetary-sized masses were collapsed by the pressure of the Bang. Hawking calculates that all black holes should end in a great explosion, the time until that explosion being related to their size. These mini holes should last about ten billion years.

And guess what? The Big Bang took place just about ten billion years ago, give or take a few billion, so these mini holes should be just about set to go off. If he's right, we should be able to see the radiation from their explosions with the proper instruments, and there are plans to start the pertinent experiments to test these ideas.

If some of these ideas about black holes as sources of explosions and energy turn out to be true, it might even be possible one day to harness them and use their energy here on earth. How? No one is sure, but when Einstein first said $E = mc^2$, no one then could visualize giant reactors providing half this country's energy, either.

So who knows?

✸ 16 ✸

But What
Are Little People
Made Of?

So there we have a remarkable scientific accomplishment, a model of stellar evolution that explained all the observations—normal Main Sequence stars like the sun, Red Giants, White Dwarfs, planetary nebulae and supernovae—and then went on to predict the existence of two new states of matter, neutron stars and black holes, which were subsequently discovered.

Fantastic, right? You'd think we'd be satisfied, wouldn't you? But a group of nuclear physicists wanted to push the model even further. As far back as 1954, when Willy Fowler took a year's leave from Cal Tech to study in Cambridge, he had been wondering about the problem of all the different atoms in the universe. If stars got their energy by fusing some atoms into others, mightn't such processes be the source of *all* the different atoms in the universe? Starting from hydrogen, with maybe some helium, mightn't it be possible for the stars to have synthesized all the other elements?

In the last few chapters we discussed how the normal energy-production processes involved in the life and death of a star result naturally in the production of elements beginning with hydrogen and ending with iron; that is, beginning with the simplest atom of one proton and electron and building up to complicated atoms with as many as twenty-eight protons, twenty-eight neutrons, and twenty-eight electrons.

But the atoms we see around us are more complicated than that. We couldn't get married, for example, in a world without gold and platinum; atoms of gold have seventy-nine protons and one hundred and eighteen neutrons, while atoms of platinum have seventy-eight protons and one hundred and seventeen neutrons. And we couldn't generate enough electricity to keep our world going if we weren't able to build reactors which generate energy by using the nuclear energy released in the fission of uranium atoms (ninety-two protons, one hundred and forty-three neutrons). And even if these heavy atoms were not important to us economically, the fact would still remain that they exist, and so our model must be able to account for them.

Of course they might have been produced somewhere else in the universe other than inside stars, but where? The tremendous temperatures needed to create new elements seem to exist only inside stars and nowhere else. So it was in the interiors of stars that Willy Fowler, together with Fred Hoyle and Margaret and Geoffrey Burbidge of Cambridge, looked for the answer to the creation of the heavier elements.

And it was inside stars, inside Red Giants and

Margaret and Geoffrey Burbidge, William Fowler, and Fred Hoyle

supernovae to be precise, that they found the answer.

Red Giants get their energy by fusing helium together to form carbon and then fusing helium with the carbon to form oxygen, then helium with the oxygen to form neon and carbon with itself to form magnesium, and helium with neon et cetera and so forth all the way up to the iron-56 nucleus. But things do not always go this precisely and regularly. Sometimes when a helium nucleus fuses with, say, a neon-22 nucleus, it does not do so exactly perfectly. The helium nucleus consists of two protons and two neutrons, and sometimes when the two nuclei fuse together the process is not complete and one of the neutrons goes slipping away. In this example instead of forming a nucleus of magnesium-26 we would form a nucleus of magnesium-25 and have one neutron wandering away by itself inside the star. A similar thing will happen in a certain fraction of many helium fusion processes, and the result is a steady stream of neutrons floating around free inside the Red Giant.

These neutrons will bounce around inside the star, bouncing off one atom after another, until finally instead of bouncing off a nucleus they will stick to it, forming a *new* nucleus with one extra neutron. If, for example, a free neutron sticks to an oxygen-16 nucleus it will form a new nucleus called oxygen-17 (because the new nucleus now has nine neutrons together with the original eight protons). Oxygen-17 is a stable isotope of oxygen. If another neutron should strike this new nucleus, perhaps a thousand years later, it will form the new isotope oxygen-18. If eventually another neutron hits this nucleus it will form the isotope oxygen-19. But here something different happens. The normal isotope of oxygen is oxygen-16, with eight protons and eight neutrons, exactly balanced. As we add more and more neutrons we finally reach the stage, at oxygen-19, where the approximate similarity of protons and neutrons becomes too far unbalanced for the nucleus to remain stable. A nucleus of eight protons and eleven neutrons is just not going to be stable. Somehow the nucleus must do something to achieve a better balance between its numbers of protons and neutrons.

Okay, if you were an unbalanced nucleus, what would you do?

Well, there's not much you can do except disintegrate, right? Like what good is a formal protest going to do? You might want to disintegrate by throwing off that last neutron and going back to the stable isotope oxygen-18. Unfortunately nuclei have rules to obey, just as everyone else does, and the emission of a neutron from a nucleus is simply not allowed. Even more unfortunately, the reasons for this rule are much too difficult for us to understand at this stage in our career; we simply have to accept it as an inviolable rule that nuclei may not disintegrate by emitting neutrons. It is absolutely *never* done, even with a letter of permission from one's parents. But the nucleus has to do *something*.

Do you remember at the beginning of this book we said that the only real difference between a neutron and a proton is its charge? In fact, we mentioned that a neutron is not a stable particle but can, under certain conditions, decay to form a proton plus an electron. This is precisely what it will do under these particular circumstances. One of the neutrons in the oxygen-19 nucleus will disintegrate into a proton plus an electron. This process is known as *beta radioactivity*, because the electron is known as a *beta* particle. It comes flying out of the atom, leaving behind one less neutron and one more proton in the nucleus. That is, oxygen-19 started with eleven neutrons and eight protons in the nucleus (Figure 18). One of the neutrons changed to a proton plus an electron. The electron is lost from the nucleus. Since the one neutron changed into a proton we now have only ten neutrons in the nucleus, but we now have nine protons instead of only eight. The mass of this nucleus, with nine protons and ten neutrons, is still nineteen, as it was before the radioactive transformation. But when we changed from eight protons to nine protons we changed from an atom of oxygen to a completely different atom. This is because atoms of any particular element are *defined* by the number of

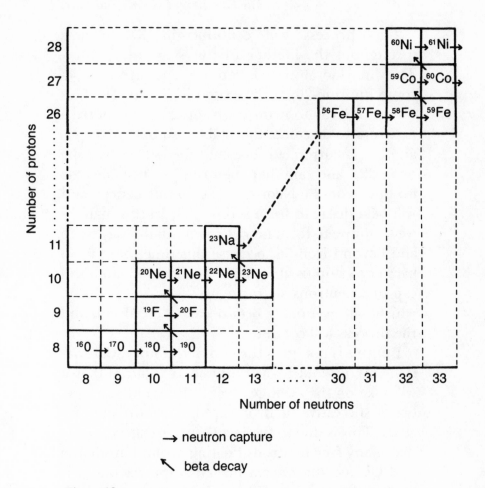

→ neutron capture

↖ beta decay

Figure 18.

protons in the nucleus. *All* atoms with eight protons are atoms of oxygen, but atoms with nine protons in the nucleus are atoms of fluorine. So the process of beta radioactivity changes oxygen-19 into fluorine-19. This whole sequence of events is illustrated in Figure 18. In this process of successive neutron-capture followed by an eventual beta decay, atoms of one element are changed into atoms of the next succeeding element.

This process will continue in Red Giants throughout the lifetime of this stage of the star. The fluorine atom will capture a neutron to become fluorine-20, as illustrated in Figure 18. This will beta-decay to neon-20. Neon-20 will capture a neutron to become the stable isotope neon-21, another neutron to become the stable isotope neon-22, and another neutron to become the isotope neon-23. Neon-23 is again unbalanced and will beta-decay to form sodium-23. In this manner we continue to form new elements all the way up to and beyond iron-56, because this time there is no barrier to stop us at iron-56. The iron-56 atom will capture neutrons to form iron-57, -58, and -59, which will eventually beta-decay to cobalt-59, and the process will continue.

But this is not quite the end of the story. Calculations carried out by astrophysicists indicate that it will take on the average several thousand years between successive neutron-captures by any one nucleus. This is due to the fact that there aren't really that many free neutrons floating around inside the Red Giants, and once a nucleus captures one it is likely to have to wait for hundreds or thousands of years before it happens to capture another one.

This leads to an interesting problem: a given nucleus will capture neutrons, leading to isotopes successively enriched in neutrons, until it reaches a point where there are too many neutrons in the nucleus to be stable. At this point the nucleus will beta-decay to form an element with one less neutron and one more proton and the process continues. The process will continue all the way up to bismuth-209, but here it comes screeching to a stop.

When bismuth-209 captures a neutron it forms bismuth-210, which will capture another neutron to form bismuth-211. This is radioactive, with a two-minute half-life, and so will decay before it has time to capture another neutron. It is radioactive, but with a different kind of radioactivity. At this point in the building up of the elements we reach atoms that are so massive they are unstable no matter *what* their relative number of neutrons and protons; the atoms are just too big to be stable. They spontaneously decay by throwing off alpha particles. These, remember, are helium nuclei, consisting of two protons and two neutrons. So when bismuth-211 (eighty-three protons) loses an alpha particle it becomes thallium-207 (eighty-one protons). This beta-decays to lead-207, which builds up again through lead-208 and -209 to bismuth-209, -210, and -211 again and we're right back where we started. Figure 19 shows this cycle, which effectively ends the process of element formation by neutron-capture.

Figure 19.

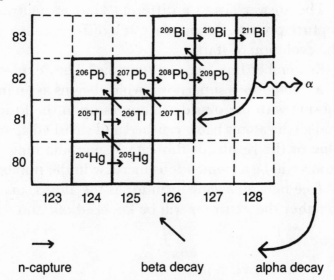

There is no way to form heavier elements since above bismuth there simply are no stable elements; there is not one single isotope that is not too heavy to exist, and so they all are radioactive and decay down to particles of lower mass by emitting alpha particles.

Well, this would not be too bad in itself. It simply means that there is an upper limit to the size of possible atoms and that above this size no further atoms will be formed. But this conclusion is not true. Atoms heavier than bismuth, although radioactive, do in fact exist. For example, the two main isotopes of uranium have ninety-two protons and one hundred and forty-three or one hundred and forty-six neutrons for a total mass of two hundred and thirty-five or two hundred and thirty-eight. As we mentioned before, we're extremely lucky that these atoms of uranium exist; we are depending upon them to an increasing extent every year for our energy production. But if the capture of neutrons in Red Giants stops at bismuth, how are these much heavier atoms of uranium ever formed?

The answer lies in a different kind of neutron-capture process, taking place at a different stage in the evolution of stars.

Remember how massive stars die? They explode in a tremendous supernova, which begins as an implosion with the outside falling in upon the inside and all the atoms being crushed and smashed apart. One of the results of this cataclysmic smashing of atoms will be a tremendous increase in the number of free neutrons lying around; as the atoms smash together the neutrons will be knocked out and will go careening throughout the imploding star. There will be such a tremendous number of neutrons flying around inside the supernova that within the space of a few seconds, or even less, one nucleus might capture fifteen or twenty or thirty or forty neutrons. The result would be to form a nucleus which is tremendously unstable with respect to the numbers of neutrons and protons but which did not have time to decay after capturing one neutron before it captured another one and another one and another after that to reach finally this very unstable state. The nuclei formed by this process will be so terribly overbalanced with neutrons as compared to protons that instead of decaying by alpha particle emission they will try first to even up the numbers of neutrons and protons by the process of beta decay, changing their overabundant neutrons into protons. The result is illustrated in Figure 20. In this example a nucleus of lead-204 has captured thirty-four neutrons to form a nucleus of lead-238. This decays successively by beta emission to form the nuclei of bismuth-238, polonium-238, astatine-238, and so on and so on and finally uranium-238.

Uranium-238 is of course much too heavy to be a stable nucleus, but its numbers of neutrons and protons are sufficiently well balanced so that it will decay by alpha emission rather than beta emission. When it does, it forms an atom of thorium-234 which is itself radioactive and will continue to alpha-decay, and the chain of decaying nuclei will continue until we're back at lead-204 (Figure 3). But it just happens that the half-life of uranium-238 is very long; 4.5 billion years. This means that

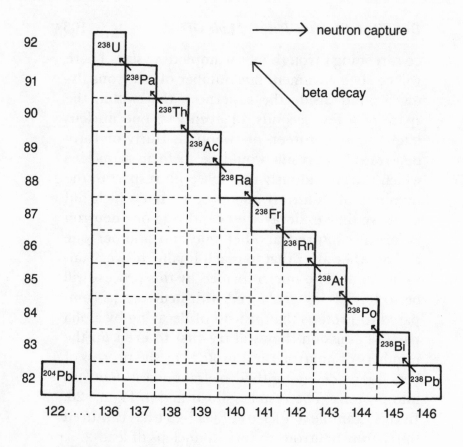

Figure 20.

of all the uranium formed by this process during a supernova, half will still remain 4.5 billion years later and half of that will still be around after another 4.5 billion years. This is about the length of time that has elapsed between now and the supernova that created these heavy elements that we now see on earth, and so a certain fraction of the uranium that was formed in that supernova still exists and is here to be found and mined on earth for our convenience. If its half-life had happened to be much less it would have decayed away before now.

And so we end up with a complete story. Starting with the universe composed of atoms in their simplest state, hydrogen, we end up by creating every other possible kind of atom, all the way up to uranium, simply by following through our model of the life and death of stars. It's kind of a weird feeling to look around us and realize that all the atoms out of which everything here on earth is made, including you and me and mosquitoes and Coca-Cola, were all created billions of years ago inside the stars far, far away.

Somewhere deep inside a giant star, unknown eons of time and parsecs of distance away from us here and now, the atoms that were ultimately to form our planet and our hair and skin and bones were being formed by the nuclear processes of fusion and neutron-capture, providing energy to light that star. After millions and billions of years the star exploded in a supernova, the exploding envelope carrying many of the complex atoms it had formed out into the universe. There the atoms dispersed and wandered throughout the vast emptiness of space until one day, by chance, they became included in a cloud of gas and dust that was condensing to form a new star. This new star would be composed not only of the primordial hydrogen and helium of the universe, but also of the debris of the exploded star. It is only in these second-generation stars—stars born out of the ashes and rubble of pre-existing stars—that the possibility for the formation of life and planets exists.

The formation of a star by its condensation from a cloud of gas and dust is a very inefficient process. Most of the atoms in the original cloud will not end up in the star but will be left behind, either floating around the star or lost again to space. If the cloud consists of at least a small percentage of the complicated and heavier atoms such as carbon, nitrogen, oxygen, silicon, and iron, then these heavier atoms may clump together to form particles which will orbit around the star. In time these particles will collide with each other and may stick together to form larger and larger bodies, eventually forming a system of planets. On these planets, if the conditions are right, the carbon compounds may begin to unite to start the life processes. But that is another story for another book.

❖ 17 ❖

Penultimento

And we're not quite finished with the whole story of this book.

Twenty years ago I graduated from the University of Florida with a Ph.D in nuclear chemistry. I had done my research at Oak Ridge, studying the nuclear disintegrations that occur when a nitrogen nucleus is smashed into a sulphur nucleus, and now I was on my way to Brookhaven National Laboratory to take up a postdoctoral position and do research in high-energy nuclear chemistry. When I got to Brookhaven, halfway out Long Island, not quite as far as Westhampton, I wandered around talking to the senior members of the staff to see what type of research they were doing and what project I might fit into most happily. One of these men was Raymond Davis, Jr., a soft-spoken, old-world southern gentleman and a nuclear chemist of great repute and ingenuity. He invited me to work on a project in which he was attempting to measure for the first time the flow of *neutrinos* from the sun. I smiled and nodded and tried to look very knowledgeable, as a recent Ph.D. should, and said I'd like to think it over. Then I went back to my desk and dug out my old textbooks to read up on neutrinos and find out just exactly what they are and why the hell they should be expected to be flowing out of the sun . . .

✳18✳

The Neutrino Triumph

Neutrinos are the cleverest little creatures in all creation. By that I don't mean that the neutrinos themselves are clever but that the *concept* of neutrinos is: the thinking up of the idea of the neutrino is one of the cleverest moments in the history of science. This was the situation in 1925:

We've talked before about beta radioactivity, in which a neutron changes into a proton and throws an electron out of the nucleus. The electron is the beta particle and carries with it the energy of the nuclear transformation. In order for one nucleus to beta-decay into another spontaneously, which means without anybody providing it with any energy to make the reaction go, the decaying nucleus must have enough energy to do the job itself. For example when oxygen-19 is to decay into fluorine-19, as we discussed earlier, the oxygen-19 nucleus must contain more energy than the flourine-19 nucleus. This difference in energy can be measured in the form of mass; the oxygen-19 nucleus actually weighs 19.0095 while the fluorine nucleus weighs only 19.0044. This difference in mass corresponds to the energy given off in the nuclear transformation. The way this energy is given off is in kinetic energy of the beta particle, the electron. It takes energy to make a particle move (any particle—an electron or a Cadillac or a 707 jet) and the more energy you give it the faster it will be moving. So back when beta radioactivity was first discovered, the next experiment to investigate what was going on was clear: measure the speed with which the beta particle comes out, and calculate from that how much energy it carries. That should tell you the energy of the nuclear transformation. If the theory is correct this should exactly equal the difference in mass between the two nuclei, in our example the oxygen-19 and fluorine-19 nuclei.

When this was done a very surprising result was obtained. Since all oxygen-19 atoms weigh *exactly* the same and all fluorine-19 atoms weigh *exactly* the same, the transformation from oxygen-19 to fluorine-19 should always involve *exactly* the same amount of energy. The electron coming out of this reaction must always have exactly the same amount of energy. In a *different* decay, between two different types of atoms, electrons of a different amount of energy should come out; but in any given reaction the electrons should always have a precise amount of energy. When scientists first measured the energy coming out of beta-radioactive processes, however, they found that electrons came out of any given reaction with a *spread* in energies. The *highest*-energy electron corresponded precisely to the amount calculated for that reaction, but most of the electrons came out with energies much less than this, ranging all the way down to zero.

This was an impressive conflict with the model which no one could understand. When oxygen-19 decays to fluorine-19 it *must* give off exactly the amount of energy corresponding to the masses of the atoms involved. If the electron carries off less energy than this, then the difference is energy which is simply lost, destroyed. But this is impossible, if we understand anything at all about science.

Well of course there are always a lot of people who are ready to jump up and down at every unexplained experiment and yell, "See, see, you *don't* know anything about science." But aside from giving these people a good shove there didn't seem to be much that anyone could do about the problem. The energy had simply disappeared.

People wondered and thought and argued about this problem for many years, and then a young Austrian physicist named Wolfgang Pauli got a very clever idea. "Look," he said, "there wouldn't be any problem at all if there were *two* particles emitted in the radioactive disintegration, would there?"

There were two answers to that question. The first answer is that no, there wouldn't be any problem, because the problem lies in the fact that the beta particle carries off the energy of the radioactive disintegration and it doesn't carry enough energy. If there were another particle and that particle carried off the missing amount of energy, then of course there would be no problem. But the second answer to that question is, "There *is* no second particle."

When Pauli asked that question and people gave him the first answer he would smile and nod his head wisely. When they gave him the second answer he said, "How do you *know* there is no second particle?"

"Because in all the experiments that have been done measuring the various properties of a nuclear disintegration, no such second particle has ever been seen. If it existed we certainly would have seen it."

"Suppose it were a very *tiny* little particle," Pauli said. "So tiny as to be virtually invisible."

"But then it still would have been *felt*." By this it was meant that there are instruments which can measure the *momentum* of a particle; this is in effect feeling the impact of the particle as it hits the instrument. No matter how tiny Pauli's new particle might be, it still had to carry a lot of energy if it were to be of any use in resolving the problem, and so when it slammed into one of these momentum-detecting instruments its impact would surely have been felt.

"Supposing it's something like a super X-ray," Pauli suggested. "Perhaps it can pass right through solid matter without interacting with it. Then it would pass right through our momentum-detection instruments and we wouldn't even know it had been there."

"In order for it to be so tiny it would have to have virtually zero mass, right?" they asked, and Pauli nodded his head.

"And in order for it to pass through our instruments without being detected it would have to have not only zero mass but it couldn't have any electric charge at all, because an electric charge passing through these instruments would certainly set them off, right?" And again Pauli nodded his head.

"So what you are suggesting is a particle with zero mass and zero charge, right?" And again Pauli nodded his head.

"But if a particle has zero mass and zero charge, then it doesn't really exist, does it? I mean, with no mass and no charge, there just isn't anything there *to* exist!"

"Perhaps," Pauli suggested, "the only way in which it can be said to exist is that it is created at the time of the nuclear disintegration and comes flying out of the nucleus carrying away the energy which the beta particle does not carry away."

It did not seem very reasonable. This sort of argument is known as an *ad hoc* argument, a couple of Latin words which mean *after the fact*. It is the sort of argument that is more prevalent in religion and politics than in science, and is usually more of an excuse than a path toward the truth. For example, the Bible told us that the universe was created in six days. When we discovered that it actually took billions of years, the *ad hoc* argument was made that well, a biblical day is just a "symbolic" term; it doesn't *really* mean twenty-four hours, not *exactly*. Maybe twenty-five or twenty-six hours or a couple of hundred million years, something like that. Or the proposition is presented that world communism is a monolithic conspiracy controlled completely by Moscow; when we find out that China and Russia are ideological enemies the *ad hoc* argument is presented that well, after all, there must be *two* monolithic worldwide communist conspiracies, one directed by Moscow and one by Peking. In each of these cases it would be much closer to the truth to simply have said that the model was wrong.

In science people do not like such *ad hoc* arguments, because the object of science is not to preserve a religious or political point of view, but somehow to get at the truth. And so instead of accepting Pauli's argument about the little invisible particles, most people continued to think that there must be something wrong with the beta-disintegration process, either with the theory or the experiments. But as the years went on nobody could find anything wrong with the theory (except for the missing energy) and as the experiments were repeated more carefully nobody could find anything wrong with *them*. The energy had simply disappeared. And time passed by, and a more complicated theory of the beta process involving Pauli's mysterious neutrinos (an Italian word meaning *tiny neutral one*) became very beautifully worked out mathematically. Little by little the neutrinos began to take on what appeared to be a valid theoretical reality of their own, even though nobody had ever seen them and nobody could figure out how they might be seen.

For the next thirty years no very great progress was made. All the experiments carried out during that time which measured various aspects of the beta-decay process found total agreement with the theory; but the theory needed the existence of neutrinos in order to avoid the disappearance of energy, and nobody was able to find these little neutrinos. Of course, the fact that nobody could find them fit in perfectly with Pauli's original description of the neutrinos: as particles without any mass or charge they must be invisible, or nearly so, and so it was natural that nobody could see them; but this argument could not be used to prove their existence. Using the same kind of reasoning you could "prove" that the world is populated by vast hordes of invisible green men: the fact that nobody has ever seen them would only prove that indeed they *are* invisible! Would you believe me if I told you that such an invisible green man was sitting on your shoulder right now as you read this, and is in fact laughing at you because you find it hard to believe in him? If you don't believe that would you believe me if I told you that a hundred thousand invisible neutrinos are whizzing through your head right this second? If you have any sense you won't believe either of those statements, but in fact at least the second one is true. I don't know about the little green men, but there are *more* than a hundred thousand neutrinos whizzing through your head every second of the day and night. You can't see them because they're invisible, and they pass right through your head without interacting or doing any damage so you can't feel them, but we know they're there because finally, about thirty years after Pauli predicted their existence, in 1956 two scientists finally found the little buggers.

According to the theory of beta decay, when a nucleus undergoes a radioactive transformation both a beta particle and a neutrino are emitted, and the resulting nucleus may be stable. It was found that the theory also predicts that the *reverse* situation should be possible: if a neutrino interacts with a stable atom it should produce a nucleus that is radioactive and which will then emit a beta particle.

In order to test this, two American scientists, Frederick Reines and Clyde Cowan, set up their equipment next to a nuclear reactor in Savannah, Georgia. A nuclear reactor produces intense beta-particle radiation, and therefore also neutrino radiation (if the neutrinos really exist). When they carried out the experiment they found that a certain number of normally stable atoms were transformed into radioactive atoms by being placed next to the reactor. The only way this could have happened was if neutrinos really were being emitted from the reactor and were interacting with the normally stable atoms, making them radioactive. This experiment finally proved the existence of Pauli's hypothetical neutrinos. Whoopee!

✹19✹

Meanwhile,
Back at the Sun

Ray Davis, the nuclear chemist at Brookhaven, read about the Reines-Cowan experiment and had an idea. To understand his idea we have to talk in a little more detail about what's actually going on inside the sun.

We have said that the sun gets its energy by fusing four hydrogen nuclei into one helium nucleus. This simple statement is a bit of an oversimplification. If you have been thinking as you read, you probably realized that there was something wrong with this description and have been wondering and worrying about it. If so, read on and worry no more. If not, go back to Go (do not collect $200).

The hydrogen nucleus consists solely of one proton. If four of them are fused together, the result would be a nucleus of four protons, but the helium nucleus has two protons and two neutrons. What actually happens is that when the four protons are fused together, two of the protons become neutrons. In the process each of the two protons emits a positive electron which carries away the positive charge and leaves these two protons as neutrons.

These positive electrons are in every way identical to the normal negatively-charged beta particles, except that their charge is positive. The process is therefore another type of beta radioactivity, and therefore neutrinos must be emitted. Since this process is the main process providing energy for the sun, and since an enormous amount of energy is involved, there must be an enormous number of neutrinos flying out from the sun. The earth, as well as being bathed in sunlight, should also be bathed in sun-neutrinos.

This was Davis's clever idea. It should be possible to set up an experiment similar to the Cowan-Reines experiment to detect these neutrinos from the sun. He set about calculating precisely how it might be done. First of all, he had to pick a stable atom that would turn into a radioactive atom that would be convenient to measure. He chose the element chlorine, which upon being hit with neutrinos from the sun should turn into radioactive argon, which Davis already knew how to measure from previous unrelated experiments. But the fraction of chlorine atoms that would actually be transformed into argon is extremely small because, as we have said before, neutrinos hardly ever react with anything. Of all the neutrinos coming out of the sun only a very very tiny fraction will actually react with the chlorine atoms.

Because such a very tiny fraction of the neutrinos will react, he wanted to pack as many chlorine atoms as possible into as small a space as possible. For this reason he decided not to use pure chlorine, which is a gas, but instead he chose ordinary cleaning fluid. The formula for this is C_2CL_4, telling us that four out of every six atoms in the cleaning fluid are chlorine; since it is a liquid instead of a gas, this enabled him to pack more chlorine atoms into his space than if he had used pure chlorine gas. Next, he took advantage of the fact that argon has a very peculiar chemical behavior. Like the other noble gases helium, neon, krypton, and xenon it does not react chemically with anything at all. Therefore any argon atom produced by the neutrino reaction on chlorine would remain as an individual atom, unbound to any of the cleaning fluid. His basic idea was simply to let a bottle of cleaning fluid sit and be hit by neutrinos for a period of time; when the time was up he would bubble some helium gas through the cleaning fluid and this helium gas would sweep out any argon atoms that had been formed. The helium would sweep the argon into a Geiger counter where the radioactivity would be counted. The amount of radioactivity produced would depend on the number of neutrinos that had passed through the solution.

But there were a couple of problems. Davis was able to estimate the number of neutrinos expected from the nuclear reactions in the sun and the fraction of these that would actually cause the reaction in the bottle of cleaning fluid. From this he was able to calculate how long he would have to let a normal bottle of cleaning fluid stand before there were enough argon atoms to count in his Geiger counter. Davis at this time had built the world's most sensitive Geiger counter for counting radioactive argon atoms; he could detect as few as one individual radioactive atom per week! Nevertheless he found that he would have to let the bottle of cleaning fluid stand for several *centuries* before enough radioactive argon was formed for him to be able to count accurately. Now Davis is a very patient scientist, but waiting a few centuries to get the results of an experiment did seem a bit too long. He was able to overcome this problem, however, by simply increasing the size of the bottle of cleaning fluid, providing more atoms for the neutrinos to hit and therefore providing more radioactive argon atoms. He calculated that in order to get a sufficient number of radioactive argon atoms within a time of about one month he would need a railroad boxcar full of cleaning fluid.

The next problem was that neutrinos are not the only things which can cause the reactions on chlorine to produce radioactive argon. *Cosmic rays* can also do it.

Cosmic rays?

✲20✲

Cosmic
Rays

Way back at the beginning of this century, at about the same time that Einstein was working out his theory of relativity and Rutherford was working out the details of radioactivity, a couple of German scientists had themselves a kind of a problem.

They were doing some experiments on the conduction of electricity, and they found the surprising result that *air* was conducting electricity. Well, they figured that this could be due to water vapor in the air. So they set up an experiment in which they dried the air thoroughly (and if you think that's easy to do, get out the best towel you have and try it) and they found that even this totally dry air continued to conduct electricity. But the neutral atoms of which air is composed have a chemical composition that should not allow such electrical conduction. They reasoned that the only way the dry air could conduct electricity was if the atoms of air were somehow being ionized; if the atoms somehow had some of their electrons knocked away. The resulting *ions* would be electrically charged and would be excellent electrical conductors. But what could be ionizing the air?

Radioactivity, obviously. One of the results of the alpha and beta particles emitted in radioactive decay is the ionization of whatever substance they travel through. If there were small amounts of radioactive substances such as potassium and uranium in the equipment used to measure the conductivity of the air, then the air in the apparatus would be continually ionized by the radioactivity and this would explain the results of the experiment. So they duplicated the experiment, being very careful to use only the purest materials they could in the construction of their apparatus, getting rid of any uranium or potassium contamination in the material. They found that the electrical conductivity of the air diminished, but did not go to zero. Clearly something was still ionizing the air inside their apparatus.

Their next guess was that the air was being ionized by radioactive materials in the earth itself. Uranium and potassium are part of the ground beneath us and this source of radioactivity would also ionize the air inside the apparatus. So they shielded their equipment in heavy blocks of lead which would absorb all the radioactive particles. Again the electrical conductivity of the air decreased, but again it did not go all the way to zero.

The answer to this, they thought, was that the lead had absorbed most of the alpha and beta particles, but not all of them. The one remaining test to prove that they were right would be to take their apparatus up in an airplane far away from the earth and see if then the conductivity of the air would actually decrease all the way to zero. Unfortunately they had this one little problem: the airplane had not yet been invented.

And so nothing more was done for a few years, until in 1911 a very brave experimental physicist named Albert Gockel took the equipment up in a balloon to check this effect. He was only able to get a few hundred feet off the ground, however, and this distance was not enough to show a meaningful change in the electrical conductivity of the air. It wasn't until the next year when two other physicists, Drs. V. F. Hess and W. Kolhorster, took the apparatus up several thousands of feet in a free-floating balloon that they found the answer to the question.

When they took the equipment up this far away from the surface of the earth, they found that the electrical conductivity of the air did *not* decrease as they had expected. In fact, it *increased*. At an altitude of about ten thousand feet the air was conducting electricity ten times as efficiently as it had on the ground!

The only way this could be interpreted was that the invisible particles causing the ionization of the air did not come from radioactive decay of materials in the surface of the earth, but came from outer space. As the particles passed through the atmosphere they would be absorbed, so there would be fewer particles at the bottom of the atmosphere (near the ground) than there would be at the top of the atmosphere. When the equipment was taken up in the balloon it had been exposed to more and more of these "cosmic rays" and the electrical conductivity of the air therefore increased.

In the years that followed the discovery of these cosmic rays many experiments were done, and we now know that the cosmic rays consist mainly of protons (hydrogen nuclei) traveling at nearly the speed of light. At these tremendous velocities they carry enormous amounts of energy, and so as they travel through the atmosphere they are capable of knocking electrons loose and thereby ionizing the air.

They are capable of a lot more than that. As they hit our bodies, which they do at roughly the rate of about one thousand every minute, they are capable of ionizing the atoms in our body and causing destruction to the chemical compounds and cells of which we are composed. This is not entirely bad, however. Some people now think that it is the influence of cosmic rays on genetic materials which causes *mutation*, and these mutations are the driving force behind evolution. In other words, if it were not for the action of these cosmic rays you and I would probably be nothing more than bacteria or cockroaches. Life, at least in its more exciting developed states, would never have evolved on this earth. Other scientists think that cosmic rays, as well as being responsible for the evolution of life, may also be responsible for the periodic extinctions of life that the earth has experienced. For example, a few hundred million years ago the earth was crawling with dinosaurs. Suddenly, in a geologic twinkling, they were gone. How? Why? What destroyed them so completely and so suddenly? As we look back through the fossil record of life on earth, we find that such extinctions of whole classes of life have not been particularly rare. Other great extinctions have occurred suddenly, and for no apparent reason.

Some scientists have suggested that a reason might be a sudden burst of cosmic rays hitting the earth. These could be due to a nearby supernova; this might very well result in a tremendous and sudden quantity of cosmic rays. Another possibility lies in the fact that we know that many cosmic rays are reflected from the earth by the earth's magnetic field, and we also know that periodically the earth's magnetic field reverses itself. If during this reversal the magnetic field disappears for a while, it is possible that the earth during this interval of zero magnetic field would be swamped by cosmic rays which are normally deflected from it, and again this sudden increase in cosmic-ray intensity on earth might have resulted in the extinction of many forms of life.

To be perfectly honest, there are a lot of arguments against these ideas. I just threw them in to get you interested in cosmic rays, because cosmic rays turn out to be an important nuisance to the neutrino experiment.

✡21✡

Back
to the Neutrino
Experiment

Cosmic rays come pouring into the earth's atmosphere with sufficient energy not only to ionize
atoms and disrupt chemical compounds but also to
disrupt the nuclei themselves, transforming them
into other nuclei. One of the particular nuclear
reactions that is possible is for a cosmic ray to trans-
form a chlorine nucleus into one of argon-37, the
same radioactive isotope of argon that Davis
wanted to measure as a test for the neutrinos. This
can happen when a cosmic-ray proton hits a nucleus of chlorine-37, knocks out a neutron, and itself gets stuck in the nucleus. The very early experiments on cosmic rays, discussed in the last chapter,
showed us that although the intensity of the cosmic
rays gets smaller and smaller as we come inside the
atmosphere, at the surface of the earth there is still
a considerable number of these rays. The probability of forming argon-37 from a cosmic-ray interaction with chlorine turns out to be much greater
than the probability of a neutrino inducing the
same result. It therefore becomes necessary to re-
move the apparatus from the possible cosmic-ray

interaction in order to see any hypothetical neutrino reactions.

For example, in the neutrino experiment Davis
expected about 50 atoms of argon-37 to be formed
each month by the neutrinos. But the cosmic rays
would probably form about 5,000 atoms per
month. Furthermore, this number might vary by
easily 10%, so that the actual number of cosmic-ray
interactions might run from 4,500 to 5,500 a
month. Then if, for example, Davis were to measure 4,800 argon-37 atoms in one month he would
not know if all 4,800 had been formed by cosmic
rays and absolutely *none* by neutrinos, or if perhaps
4,750 had been formed by cosmic rays and the expected 50 by neutrinos, or if in fact only 4,500 had
been formed by cosmic rays and an exceptional 300
had been formed by neutrinos. In order to measure
the neutrino-produced argon accurately he had to
get rid of the cosmic-ray background.

Unfortunately there is no switch in the sky which
one can flip to turn off the cosmic rays. The only
answer was to move the equipment somewhere so
that the cosmic rays could not follow. But they are
everywhere on the surface of the earth. The answer
was clear. The experiment must be carried out
somewhere else other than on the surface of the
earth.

All in all, it doesn't sound like an easy experiment, does it? It didn't to me at the time. The way I
looked at it, it seemed like one of the toughest
radiochemical experiments ever thought up, involving the setup of a whole tank-car of volatile,
flammable, poisonous C_2Cl_4 somewhere not on the
surface of the earth—which meant down in a mine

or a submarine or somewhere equally yucky—and involving months of waiting for neutrino events to accumulate and then more months counting the radioactive gas. It meant working to a precision not yet attained in more normal experiments, under conditions where one careless slip would mean either wiping out all those months of careful, tedious work or, more likely, falling into that tank-car of poisonous cleaning fluid . . .

And at the end of it, what would we have accomplished? We would have detected the neutrinos flowing out of the sun. Well, I mean, so what? We *knew* neutrinos were flowing out of the sun—we could even calculate pretty exactly what the flux must be. Of course it's always important to check such calculations experimentally, but the experiments are fun only when there's a good chance of proving the calculations wrong, of catching the theorists in a mistake. In this particular case, there didn't seem to be much chance of that. The theory was too solidly entrenched to allow room for any serious error. The theory accounted for just about everything we could observe, all the different kinds of stars and all the different kinds of atoms. It *couldn't* be wrong.

So I told Ray Davis thank you for the invitation, but no thank you. I decided that the likely results of the experiment just weren't worth all the hard work it was going to entail, and I picked another project to work on. And that's how I missed being involved in the most exciting radiochemical experiment since the discovery of nuclear fission.

✡22✡

The Neutrino Disaster

Davis pressed on. He talked to the owners of the Homestake gold mine in Lead, South Dakota. When he explained the importance of the experiment they agreed to set aside space for him two-thousand feet under the ground. The cosmic rays would not be able to penetrate two-thousand feet of solid earth. A diagram of the experiment is shown in Figure 21. The tank-carload of poisonous inflammable cleaning fluid was carefully lowered down into the mine and set in place. All the supporting equipment was very carefully set up around it. Day after day and night after night the tank-car full of cleaning fluid sat there, shielded from cosmic rays, hopefully bathed in a shower of neutrinos which were created in the center of the sun, had passed right through the two-thousand feet of earth in daytime and through the other 4×10^7 feet of earth in the nighttime and hurtled through the target atoms (Figure 21). At the end of each month Davis bubbled some helium through the tank-car to sweep out any radioactive argon that might have been formed. He was looking each

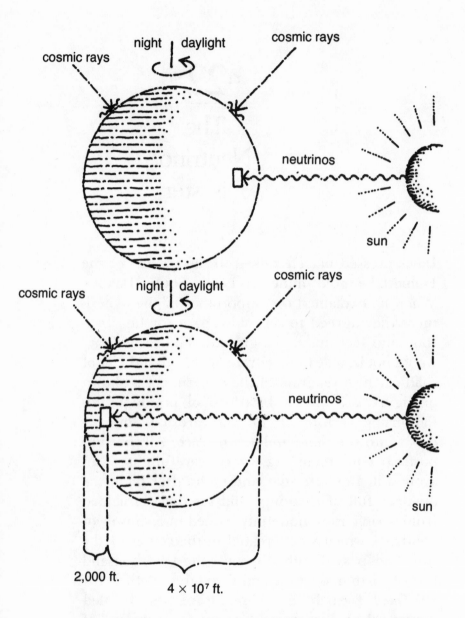

Figure 21. At the top, the tank of C_2Cl_4 buried in the Home-stake mine in South Dakota is on the daylight side of the earth. At the bottom, the earth has spun so that it is night in South Dakota, but the neutrinos from the sun travel right through the whole earth and still hit their target.

month for about fifty argon atoms from a background of about 10^{30} chlorine atoms.

He didn't find them. Each month he collected the
helium gas he had bubbled through the tank together with the argon atoms that he hoped it contained, and brought it back to Brookhaven. There
he inserted the gas into his specially designed
Geiger counter, about as small as your thumb. He
then hooked this up to a complicated apparatus
which would screen out any kind of count except
those due to the radioactive argon-37 atoms and
then he sat down and waited for the argon-37
atoms to disintegrate and their counts to be re-
ported in the counter. He waited and he waited.

And month after month the counts were not
there. The fifty argon atoms per month were simply not there. Again and again he went over the
details of his experiment, changing little things
here and there in an effort to find out what could
possibly be going wrong. But nothing he could
think of, nothing he could do, made any difference.
He was not finding the fifty argon atoms that
should have been produced every month by the
neutrinos from the sun because they just weren't
there. Which meant that, somehow, unbelievable as
it seemed to be, the solar neutrinos that *must* be
produced in the fusion of hydrogen in the sun just
aren't produced.

Month after month went by, year after year, and
still there were no neutrinos. Knowing that the
neutrinos had to be there, and therefore that the
argon-37 atoms had to be produced, Davis did not
announce his results but continued to check and
recheck his experiments. Finally, ten years after he

had begun, he was convinced that there was no fault in the experiment. If the argon-37 atoms had been produced he would have seen them. And so, finally, he announced his results.

It was very difficult for the theoreticians who had so painstakingly constructed the very detailed model of the solar interior to take him seriously. The neutrinos simply *had* to be there, and so, while they began to worry and wonder over how the model might be patched up to account for the missing neutrinos, Davis went back to his experiment in an attempt to measure what was going on even more accurately, with even less risk of error.

In any experiment there is always some error. If you turn on the radio and someone tells you that at the sound of the chime it will be twelve-thirty, it might actually be ten seconds after or before twelve-thirty. If a map tells you that the distance between Hartford and New York City is one hundred and ten miles, you can't be sure that it isn't one hundred and ten miles plus one foot. With every measurement of time or space or anything at all, there is always the possibility of an error. If you took thirty cards out of a deck of playing cards and counted them you might get exactly the right number, but you might not. If you ask twenty people to count those cards I bet not everybody would come up with the same answer. And in any scientific experiment there is always the same possibility of error. But if the experiment is designed properly and repeated sufficiently often, the amount of the possible error can be accurately estimated. In 1976, more than fifteen years after he began his experiment, Davis announced that he had not yet found any definite evidence for solar neutrinos, and that the error in his experiments was such that the *most* argon atoms that possibly could have been produced was about ten per month instead of the fifty everyone had expected. There could be no more than one fifth the calculated number of neutrinos being produced in the sun.

❊23❊

Back to the
Old Drawing Board

The neutrino experiment carried out by Ray Davis has shot down in flames our model of what is going on inside the sun. Yet the model is so simple and reasonable in conception that it has an innate beauty we would hate to loose. To describe a phenomenon as overwhelming as the sun we say simply that a cloud of gas and dust contracts under its own gravitational pressure, and the energy released by this process causes the hydrogen to fuse into helium. This releases thermonuclear energy which keeps the sun burning for ten billion years. When the hydrogen in the core is finally used up, further gravitational contraction will start the helium fusing together to form carbon, and the sun will enter a new stage. During all this time, neutron-capture processes are forming all the other elements. Eventually the star implodes, explodes, and contracts to its final death.

Each step in this model follows logically and simply from the previous one, and yet despite its simplicity the model has accounted successfully for all the observed properties of all the different stars in the skies, and has even predicted other properties and types of stars that had not yet been observed.

For example, first of all, the model has enabled us to account for the great age of the sun (Chapter Two). There is no means of energy generation that will last for billions of years except nuclear energy produced by the fusion of nuclei into successively heavier nuclei. Second, a thermonuclear reaction which is initiated by heat generated by gravitational attraction is the only mechanism which can account for the balance required so that the reaction rate remains reasonably constant over the billion-year time periods involved (Chapter Nine).

Next, it accounts for the three major classes of stars: the Main Sequence, the Red Giants, and the White Dwarfs (Chapters Eleven and Twelve). It tells us why most of the stars are Main Sequence stars; since a star on the Main Sequence will remain there for ten to a thousand times longer than in the Red Giant or White Dwarf stages, it follows naturally that most of the stars we observe will be on the Main Sequence. It gives a perfectly reasonable explanation for the existence of such astronomical objects as the Crab Nebula and tells us why there "just happens" to be a pulsar at the exact center of the crab (Chapter Thirteen).

Even more impressive, and quite impossible to imagine simply as mere coincidences, are the predictions that the theory has made of astronomical objects which had never been seen before. The model had been telling us for years that such things as neutron stars must exist. Finally the pulsars were discovered and we realized that these objects must be the long-sought neutron stars (Chapter Fifteen). Most marvelous of all, because these are such mysterious and exotic objects, is first the prediction and then the observation of the black hole (Chapters Fourteen and Fifteen).

And then there is technetium. Technetium is an element with no stable isotopes; like uranium it is completely radioactive. Unlike uranium, however, the half-life of its most stable isotope is only a few million years. Because of this there is no technetium on earth; any technetium initially present when the earth was formed has long since decayed and disappeared. The same must be true of any Main Sequence stars: if any technetium was present when the star first formed it would have decayed away and disappeared by the time the star reached the Main Sequence, *unless* it is being produced continually by nuclear processes in the stars. Astronomers therefore carefully looked for the spectral lines of technetium in the light coming to us from stars, and they have found it! If it exists today in stars, the conclusion is inescapable that it must be being continually produced in these stars.

Overall the evidence that nuclear reactions are taking place in stars and are in fact responsible for the energy of these stars is overwhelming, and yet it is clear from the Davis experiment that the neutrinos that must accompany these reactions are simply not present. Somehow we must account for the absence of these neutrinos without throwing away the stellar nuclear model which has proven to be so successful. This is not an easy thing to do, and so the ideas that have emerged when the astronomers and astrophysicists went back to their pencils and calculators have been sometimes rather wild and at all times extremely controversial.

Willie Fowler, at Cal Tech, one of the founders and chief architects of this whole business of stellar nuclear models, has come out with the suggestion that perhaps the sun hiccups. By this he means that while the sun sits up there pouring out energy at a steady rate for billions of years, perhaps it isn't really all that steady. Perhaps the sun gives an occasional cosmic hiccup, in which the normal rate of nuclear reactions ceases or drastically closes down momentarily.

If in fact the nuclear engine in the core of the sun were to suddenly cease entirely, what would happen? Would the sky suddenly go dark? No, it wouldn't, because the energy produced at the center of the sun does not flow directly and instantaneously from there to us. Instead the light and heat bounces around inside the tremendous mass of the sun for perhaps a million years before gradually fighting their way to the surface and then zooming across space to us as sunlight. If the nuclear engine in the center of the sun were to stop while you are reading this, you wouldn't know it for about a million years because the light falling on you today is the result of the nuclear reactions that have been taking place inside the sun over the *past* million years; the light and heat already produced in the sun would continue to emerge from the surface for roughly a million years after the sun stopped functioning.

But the neutrinos in the sun do not suffer from the same fate. The reaction of neutrinos with matter is so slight that they flip right out of the sun as soon as they are produced. Therefore if the nuclear energy at the center of the sun were to stop right now, although the sunlight would continue to come out, the neutrinos would suddenly cease. Perhaps, Fowler says, this is what is happening. The sun is not producing energy today and therefore not producing neutrinos, but the energy it has produced over the past million years enables it to continue shining.

If this were true the consequences for the future and past of the earth are tremendous. Although the sun continues to shine today with the energy of past years it will not continue indefinitely. Eventually a time will be reached when the energy that should have been produced today should have reached the surface and should shine as sunlight on the earth. At such a time in the future the sun will begin to dim and temperatures on earth will begin to fall drastically. Rapidly the waters on the earth will begin to freeze and the surface will be covered with great sheets of ice.

Has such a thing ever happened to the earth? Yes, it has. We know by studying the past history of the earth that there have been times in our history when the temperature dropped sufficiently to enable great sheets of ice to cover most of the surface of the earth. Not the entire surface, or life would have been totally destroyed, and we have mentioned before that this has never happened. But there have been times, called Ice Ages, when much of the earth's surface was covered with ice and was inhospitable to life. Perhaps, Fowler suggests, these Ice Ages are due to previous solar hiccups. Unfortunately the time scale with which these Ice Ages have invaded the earth is not the same as we would expect from such solar hiccups, and so Fowler's theory is not regarded by many scientists as likely to be true.

Fred Hoyle, another one of the pioneering group of nuclear astrophysicists, has come up with another suggestion to explain the neutrino result. He says that perhaps the sun originally formed untold billions of years ago at only half its present size. Then, 4.6 billion years ago, at the time of the creation of our solar system, the outer layers of the sun were added to the original proto-sun. The original first half of the sun was formed of different elements than those comprising the second-half addition. This type of sun, chemically heterogeneous, would have internal properties that would make it possible for only a small percentage of the neutrinos to be produced. Needless to say, this suggestion is just as exotic as Fowler's, and is not regarded by most people as any more likely to be true.

But nothing more reasonable has been suggested. Other people's ideas seem even wilder. For example, one group has calculated that if there were a tiny black hole at the center of the sun, comprising only one thousandth of 1% of the mass of the sun, it would be able to produce about half the total observed energy of the sun. This means that only half as many neutrinos as theoretically calculated would actually be produced, therefore bringing the calculations back into line with Davis's experiment, or nearly so.

Niels Bohr, at the beginning of this century, said that the trouble with most physical theories is that they are not crazy enough to be true. Nevertheless most people feel that these theories to account for the neutrino experiment seem much too crazy to be true. Instead, most physicists seem to feel that astronomers simply don't know as much about stars as they always pretended and that the neutrino experiment proves this more than anything else. A lot of astronomers, on the other hand, are wondering if perhaps the physicists don't know quite as much about the basic laws of physics as they think they do; perhaps our problem is not in a lack of knowledge of the application of nuclear reactions to the interior of stars, but to a lack of knowledge of what is actually happening during these nuclear reactions themselves. Perhaps the stars, through the neutrino experiment, are pointing the way to a better understanding of the basic laws of physics.

✧24✧

Where
Do We Go
from Here?

So anyhow, here we stand on the earth, looking up at the stars and measuring their light and their wave lengths and their colors and their temperatures and their lack of neutrinos, wondering what it all means.

An experimental result, such as the lack of neutrinos, that defies explanation through the theoretical models that we think we understand is always a cause for rejoicing rather than despair. It's happened before, time and time again, and every time when the puzzle was solved it brought forward a new jump in our understanding of the natural world around us.

Right now we don't know why the neutrinos aren't there. We don't even know if perhaps, as Shakespeare wrote, the fault "is not in our stars but in ourselves," but we do know that the problem won't last forever. Sooner or later one of the men or women working on the problem will find the answer. Or perhaps, as often happens, someone working on an entirely different problem will stumble across the answer to this one. And when the answer does come we will know a little bit more about the sun and the stars and the history and future of our universe.

Or perhaps a whole lot more.

Definitions

Atom: one of the minute, invisible particles which make up the universe. Atoms are composed of three parts: electrons, neutrons, and protons (see below).

Einstein: noun (German), one stone.

Electron, neutron, and proton: the three parts of an atom. *Neutrons* and *protons* fit together in the *nucleus* or center of the atom while the *electrons* spin in an orbit outside of the nucleus.

Extraterrestrial: originating or existing outside the earth, as extraterrestrial life would be life that exists on other planets.

Fossil: any physical object that remains of a previous form of life. A shell might be a fossil of an animal which once lived in the sea and used that shell as a home. Fossils are essential in helping to date the ages at which these animals lived.

Gravitational energy: energy released by something as it falls. For example, it takes energy to carry a stone up a mountain, so a stone on top of a mountain has more energy than one at the bottom. As the stone falls off the mountain it gives

up this gravitational energy, which may be released as heat when it hits the ground. In the case
of astronomy, gravitational energy is important
because it is released by all the particles forming a
star as they fall in towards the star's center, giving
off heat.

Hydrologic cycle: process by which fresh water is cycled continuously between the lakes and oceans,
while salt that is fed into the ocean remains there.

Implosion: an explosion directed inwardly. It is the
process by which the core of a star collapses before exploding into a supernova.

Ionization: process by which atoms lose or gain electrons.

Isotope: an atom which behaves the same as another
atom of the same chemical element, but has a
different atomic weight. The two atoms have the
same number of *protons* and *electrons*, but different numbers of *neutrons*.

Mutations: changes in genes which affect hereditary
traits and sometimes influence the process of
evolution.

Neutrinos: tiny, invisible particles given off during
beta radioactivity (see below). They carry the
energy that the beta particles can't carry.

Neutron: see electron.

Neutron Star: the remains of a supernova whose
atoms have become so compressed that the electrons have merged with the protons to form neutrons; the star is composed solely of those
neutrons.

Nucleus: see electron.

Optical spectrometer: instrument which measures the
different wave lengths in a beam of light. It is

essential for discovering what kind of atoms a star is made of.

Proton: see electron.

Pulsar: a neutron star. We see it as a source of pulsating radio waves.

Quantum theory: a theory in physics that describes the behavior of atoms and the interactions between matter and energy.

Quasars: star-like objects that shine with unusual brightness. What they really are and what the source of their energy is is still unknown.

Radioactivity: the process by which some elements give off alpha and beta particles and change from one kind of atom into another.

Repulsive force: when two positively charged particles approach each other, this electric barrier arises to push them apart.

Stable atom: atoms which remain the same forever unless subjected to external change.

Supernova: an exploding star. Its core becomes so hot that too much energy is released and the nuclear reaction runs out of control.

Theoretical model: a mental picture, idea, or explanation which suggests how a particular phenomenon works when that phenomenon cannot be observed firsthand.

Velocity: speed or rate of occurrence. Velocity of light is the speed at which light travels.

Suggestions
for Further
Reading

Fisher, David E., *Creation of the Universe.* Indianapolis: Bobbs-Merrill, 1977.
The precursor of the present book, dealing with our attempts to discover how and when the universe was created.

Clayton, Donald D., *The Dark Night Sky.* New York: Quadrangle Books, 1975.
An excellent, personal story of a cosmologist's life.

Hoyle, Fred, *Highlights in Astronomy.* San Francisco: W. H. Freeman, 1975.
Beautifully illustrated account of various astronomical subjects.

Burbidge, E. M.; Burbidge, G. R.; Fowler, William A.; and Hoyle, F., *Synthesis of the Elements in Stars* published in *Reviews of Modern Physics,* Vol. 29, pg. 548–650, 1957.
Known to a generation of astrophysicists as B^2FH or "The Bible," this is the first comprehensive account of stellar nucleosynthesis, the creation of the elements in stars. Although it was written strictly for research scientists, it's worthwhile taking at least a quick look at it to get an idea of how detailed the theory really is. It's a classic paper in science and should be available at your library.

Wade, Nicholas, *Discovery of Pulsars: A Graduate Student's Story* published in *Science,* Vol. 189, pg. 358, 1975.
The story of why Jocelyn Bell did not get the Nobel Prize.

Bahcall, J. N. and Davis, R., Jr., *Solar Neutrinos: A Scientific Puzzle* published in *Science,* Vol. 191, pg. 264–267, 1976.

A review, written for scientists, of the latest results in the neutrino puzzle story.

Field, G. B.; Verschuur, G. L.; and Ponnamperuma, C., *Cosmic Evolution*. Boston: Houghton Mifflin, 1978.
One of the better-written introductory college-level texts in astronomy. It won't be easy to work your way through this, but it can be done and it would be worth it.

Einstein, Albert, *Die Grundlage der Allgemeinen Relativitatstheorie* published in *Annalen der Physik*, Vol 49, pg 769, 1916.
Go ahead, I dare you.

Index